Heart- and Soul-Like Constructs across Languages, Cultures, and Epochs

T0373694

All languages and cultures appear to have one or more "mind-like" constructs that supplement the human body. Linguistic evidence suggests they all have a word for *someone*, and another word for *body*, but that doesn't mean that whatever else makes up a human being (i.e. someone) apart from the body is the same everywhere. Nonetheless, the (Anglo) mind is often reified and thought of in universal terms. This volume adds to the literature that denounces such reification. It looks at Japanese, Longgu (an Oceanic language), Thai, and Old Norse-Icelandic, spelling out, in a culturally neutral Natural Semantic Metalanguage (NSM), how the "mind-like" constructs in these languages differ from the Anglo mind.

Bert Peeters is an Honorary Associate Professor at the Australian National University, Canberra; an Adjunct Associate Professor at Griffith University, Brisbane; and editor of *Semantic primes and universal grammar* (2006) and *Language and cultural values: adventures in applied ethnolinguistics* (2015). His research interests are French linguistics and Natural Semantic Metalanguage.

Routledge Studies in Linguistics

For more information about this series, please visit: https://www.
routledge.com/Routledge-Studies-in-Linguistics/book-series/
SE0719

Heart- and Soul-Like Constructs across Languages, Cultures, and Epochs

Edited by Bert Peeters

Routledge
Taylor & Francis Group
New York London

First published 2019
by Routledge
605 Third Avenue, New York, NY 10017

and by Routledge
2 Park Square, Milton Park, Abingdon, Oxon OX14 4RN

First issued in paperback 2021

*Routledge is an imprint of the Taylor & Francis Group, an
informa business*

Library of Congress Cataloging-in-Publication Data
Names: Peeters, Bert, 1960– editor.
Title: Heart- and soul-like constructs across languages,
cultures, and epochs / Bert Peeters.
Description: New York; London: Routledge, [2019] |
Series: Routledge studies in linguistics; 20 |
Includes bibliographical references and index.
Identifiers: LCCN 2018051845 | ISBN 9781138745308 (hardback)
Subjects: LCSH: Ethnopsychology—Cross-cultural studies. |
Psycholinguistics—Cross-cultural studies. |
Language and culture—Cross-cultural studies.
Classification: LCC GN502 .H43 2019 | DDC 155.8/2—dc23
LC record available at https://lccn.loc.gov/2018051845

ISBN 13: 978-1-03-209394-9 (pbk)
ISBN 13: 978-1-138-74530-8 (hbk)

Typeset in Times New Roman
by codeMantra

Contents

Preface and Acknowledgements

Cultural differences in ideas about the make-up of the human person and about our "inner life" have a strong human interest dimension. This book, which is situated at the crossroads of linguistics, anthropology, and ethnopsychology, seeks to raise further awareness of the multiplicity of ways in which humans construct the nonphysical part of their beings. We all have a body, but what else do we have that makes us uniquely human? Different cultures look at this in many different ways, some of which are known better than others. More than ever before, we need to open up to how other cultures (historical as well as present) perceive personhood.

All five chapters use the same consistent and accessible methodology, which is explained in the first. It is a methodology that is grounded in linguistic evidence and that has stood the test of time. It is brought to bear on examples from a range of languages and cultures, including Japanese, Longgu (Solomon Islands), Thai, and Old Norse-Icelandic. This is the first time the methodology has been brought to bear on the topic of personhood over a number of chapters all brought together in a single volume.

The journey has been a long one, for the editor and the contributors alike. The editor wishes to thank all contributors for their patience, and particularly for putting up with his exacting requirements. Thanks are also extended to the peer reviewers, who have helped shape this volume in more ways than one. All chapters went through multiple extra revisions, even after the review process; for this, only the editor bears responsibility.

The psychological vocabulary of present-day English
does not cut nature at the joints.

(Colin Peter Mackenzie)

1 Delving into Heart- and Soul-Like Constructs
Describing EPCs in NSM

Bert Peeters

1 Delving into Heart- and Soul-Like Constructs

As a child growing up in Belgium, I was taught to sing the Belgian national anthem. Being Flemish, I was taught the Flemish version, which starts as follows:

> *O dierbaar België, o heilig land der vaad'ren,*
> *Onze ziel en ons hart zijn u gewijd [...]*

Little did I know that, 50 years on, and 30 years after migrating to Australia, I would find these words, which I have translated at the end of the paragraph, extremely helpful as a way into this introductory chapter on "heart- and soul-like constructs" (a label that is intended to cover "mind-like constructs" as well). Because that is exactly what *ziel* and *hart* in the second line are: *ziel* is usually translated as 'soul', and *hart* as 'heart', but neither can be deemed, without thorough verification, to be identical in meaning to either *soul* or *heart*, even though upon closer examination they may well turn out to be. *Ziel* is a "soul-like construct", like *Seele* in German, *sjæl* in Danish, *âme* in French, *duša* (*душа*) in Russian, etc. *Hart*, in its nonphysical meaning, is a "heart-like construct", like *Herz* in German, *hjerte* in Danish, *cœur* in French, *serdce* (*сердце*) in Russian, etc. The second line of the Flemish version of the Belgian national anthem says *something* like this: 'Our soul and our heart are devoted to you' – *you* being the 'cherished Belgium, the holy land of the fathers' referred to in the first line.

The phrase *something like this* is crucial: *ziel* and *hart*, *soul* and *heart*, are not entities that are out there (or rather "in there"), lending themselves to direct observation, detailed measurement, and minute comparison. The word that was used just now is *construct*: they are constructs, *cultural* constructs, not made with tools and tangible materials. The names we set aside for those cultural constructs are part of the psychological vocabulary of present-day Dutch and present-day English, respectively.

1.1 Ethnopsychological Words and Constructs

Words that are part of the psychological vocabulary of a language are generally speaking *unique* to that language, even though, semantically speaking, they may well be closely related to similar-sounding words in neighbouring languages. We might call them, for that very reason, "*ethno*psychological words", and the constructs they name are "ethnopsychological constructs".

In the published transcript of a lecture delivered at the end of 2016 at an international forum on Cognitive Linguistics in Beijing, the Australian linguist Cliff Goddard (2018: 168) describes ethnopsychological words as follows:

> Words that we call *ethnopsychological* are basically words for parts of a person: not the physical body, but the inside. In English, we have the word *mind*, it's a very English-specific word actually. Russian does not have a word for 'mind', not really, but Russian has its word *duša*, a very famous word [that means] something like "soul". [...] Chinese has *xīn* 心, Japanese *kokoro*, Korean *maum*. These words are not equivalent to one another.

Mind is arguably the English language's most salient ethnopsychological word; it refers to the most important nonphysical part of a person, at least from an Anglo point of view,[1] followed by *heart*, *spirit*, and *soul* – though not necessarily in that order. *Duša* is probably just as salient for the Russians, *xīn* 心 for the Chinese, *kokoro* for the Japanese, and *maum* for the Koreans, but that does not make them identical, as Goddard rightly stresses. They are in fact different, *very* different.

Anthropologists, on the other hand, talk not about ethnopsychological *words* but about ethnopsychological *categories* or *constructs*, which are of course the categories or constructs *behind* the words. The terms have been around for a while; one linguist who, over the course of her readings of the work of several anthropologists of the 1980s, came across the terms and has since adopted them in her own publications is Goddard's colleague and close collaborator Anna Wierzbicka, whose name – together with Goddard's – is synonymous with the "Natural Semantic Metalanguage approach", usually abridged to "NSM" or "NSM approach" (in this book, to distinguish the metalanguage from the approach that takes its name, we will use compounds such as the latter; for details, see Section 3). Wierzbicka (1989) may well be the first paper by a linguist to use the term *ethnopsychological category*, which the author appears to have borrowed from Schieffelin (1985). Several other scholars are mentioned, but it is a footnote of Schieffelin's, in which he draws attention to "the problem of the reification of essentially Western ethnopsychological categories that are then taken as the conceptual foundation of scientific inquiry" (Schieffelin, 1985: 127), that she quotes (Wierzbicka, 1989: 46).[2] The expanded 1992 version of Wierzbicka's paper also refers to "ethnopsychological categories and constructs"; this is probably where, as far as the NSM approach is concerned, the origins of the term *ethnopsychological construct* lie.

From Wierzbicka's writings, the term *ethnopsychological construct* spread into other NSM literature, where it has been used by several authors turning their attention to mind-, heart-, and soul-like words in a host of other languages (see Appendix A). *Ethnopsychological construct* is now an established term in NSM circles – much more so than *ethnopsychological word, ethnopsychological concept, ethnopsychological entity*, or *ethnopsychological term*, none of which are as commonly used. They are all interchangeable, though. In Goddard's (2015: 387) definition, for instance, ethnopsychological *constructs* are "*nominal expressions* [emphasis added, B.P.] designating non-physical parts of a person, akin to English *mind, heart, soul*, and *spirit*". Defining a construct as a nominal expression is tantamount to blurring the boundaries between word and concept, which is not always good practice; however, it does not matter much here since the focus is not so much on form as on meaning.

Strangely enough, among linguists, only NSM practitioners, as they have come to call themselves,[3] seem to be using the term *ethnopsychological construct*. Nowhere is this more obvious than in Sharifian et al. (2008), a watershed volume on ethnopsychological constructs approached from a linguistic point of view, in which the subset of authors using the NSM approach (Goddard, 2008; Yoon, 2008) corresponds rigorously to the subset of authors using the term *ethnopsychological construct*.

1.2 Personhood Constructs

There is another term that has found favour in NSM circles, particularly in the latest writings of Danish linguist Carsten Levisen. Levisen talks about *personhood constructs*, a term that clearly corresponds to the *ethnopsychological constructs* of other NSM authors. Indeed, for Levisen (2017: 123), *personhood* is a

> terminological shortcut for semantic concepts in natural languages which meet the following criteria: they all conceptualize (or reify) something and this something is a part of a person, but which cannot be seen by people, and often stands in contrast to the body.

Thus, in a co-authored paper (Levisen & Jogie, 2015: 169), he investigates the "personhood construct *mind* in Trinidadian creole" and refers to some recent studies on "Japanese, Malay, Korean, and Thai personhood constructs" that have "further questioned the Anglophone stronghold of 'the mind'" (*ibid.*: 170); Levisen (2017), on the other hand, deals with personhood constructs in the author's own language, Danish.

The term *personhood* enjoys a certain popularity among philosophers (Torchia, 2007; Palmquist, 2010) and those who straddle the boundary between psychology and philosophy (Scott, 1990; Harré, 1998), but it is not clear who has been Levisen's primary source of inspiration. What is clear, though, is that *personhood constructs*, like *ethnopsychological constructs*, are cultural, linguistic, and conceptual in nature (Levisen, 2017: 120–121).

1.3 Ethnopsychological Personhood Constructs

The editor of and contributors to the current volume do not, for a number of reasons, refer to "*ethnopsychological* constructs" (or "categories"), nor to "*personhood* constructs", but they want to have a foot in each camp, so to speak, and they talk about "*ethnopsychological personhood* constructs" or EPCs. The term *ethnopsychological* is retained because we want to acknowledge the work done in this area by ethnopsychologists such as Dorothy Holland, Catherine Lutz, Michelle Rosaldo, Edward Schieffelin, and Geoffrey White, to name but a few. With the term *personhood*, we want to salute the work carried out within the NSM approach by Carsten Levisen, who prefers the noun *personhood* to the adjective *ethnopsychological*; at the same time, we want to clarify that emotions, for instance, which on the face of it also qualify as 'ethnopsychological constructs', are not our main focus (even though it is impossible to talk about personhood constructs without at the same time touching on culturally specific emotions). Finally, we want to refer to *constructs* because, although it may seem like a minor terminological distraction, that term is arguably doing a better job than the term *category* at highlighting culture-specificity, something the prefix *ethno-* is supposed to emphasize as well.

2 Reification and Anglocentrism

If words such as *mind, duša, xīn, kokoro,* and *maum,* to limit ourselves to the examples in Goddard's (2018) definition of *ethnopsychological words,* are so different, how can we make sense of them? How do we describe in what ways they differ and what they have in common?

For many in today's day and age, these questions do not arise anymore (if they ever did). The dominance of English as the international *lingua franca* has led them to the assumption that *all* humans have hearts and minds. We may not all have souls, and those who "question the ontological status of 'the soul'" (Levisen & Jogie, 2015: 169) may even come to the conclusion that no one does, but the word *mind* in particular is taken for granted: Anglo scholars "pan-humanize the underlying concept and talk about it as if it existed per se, roaming in a non-linguistic, a-cultural space" (*ibid.*: 169–170). They "publish on 'how the mind works', on 'the mind and the brain', on 'body and mind', etc., as if 'the mind' was an obvious and apparently natural feature of the human setup" (*ibid.*: 170; see also Levisen, 2018). And it gets worse. Not only humans are presumed to have minds; animals – or at least certain animals – are as well. According to the publisher's blurb for Hayes (2018), "at birth, the minds of human babies are only subtly different from the minds of newborn chimpanzees". How would we know? Who has ever *seen* or *touched* the mind of a human baby? Who has ever *seen* or *touched* the mind of a newborn chimpanzee? Who can tell once and for all that all human babies and all newborn chimpanzees even *have* a mind? The reality is that not all of them do. The mind is not something out there (or, as I quipped, "in there") that lends itself to direct observation. It is a construct of present-day English. To ignore this – as many do, even though they may think they are culturally aware – is equivalent to turning a blind eye to cultural diversity. And what if the Danes, for instance, started reifying their *sind*? How would Anglo scholars react? Levisen (2012: 75), himself a Dane, offers a sobering assessment:

> The claim that speakers of all languages have a *sind* (with all its peculiar ethnopsychological implications) would obviously be blatantly Dano-centric, but so is Anglophone linguists' and psychologists' talk about "the human *mind*", as if the English concept corresponds to objective reality whether or not speakers of other languages share the concept with speakers of English.

Of course, not everyone is as blind to cultural diversity as the individuals referred to earlier. However, the vast majority of them still uncritically rely on the tools provided by their own language or by the language they use in their writing, which is more often than not the English language. In other words, those of us who are conscious of cultural differences may nonetheless form the view that English words such as *heart, soul*, and *mind* can be used, without the slightest danger, to talk about the EPCs of other languages and other cultures, no matter how different they are. Three decades ago, Wierzbicka (1989: 46, revised as 1992: 40) cautioned against this approach as follows, again with reference to the English word *mind*:

> The idea that *mind* is a folk concept reflected in the English language rather than an objective and universally valid category of human thought may seem surprising, if not impertinent. It is relatively easy to see that concepts such as those encoded in the Japanese words *kokoro* or *ki* [...], in the Samoan word *loto* [...], or in the Ilongot word *rinawa* [...] are culture-specific. It is harder to realize, however, that the same applies to the concept encoded in the English word *mind*.

The same point has since been reiterated on numerous occasions, either by Wierzbicka herself or by a handful of others. Some people have started listening, many more have not; the message still bears repeating. Large numbers of scholarly publications remain oblivious to the danger involved in taking English constructs such as the heart and the mind as universally shared yardsticks, seemingly utterly convinced that the use of English words and concepts to get to the bottom of words and concepts such as *xin* in Chinese, *hati* in

Indonesian and Malay, and *del* in Persian, to add a few more to the list, is entirely unproblematic. Little has changed since, ten years ago, Goddard (2008: 79) noted that "with a few exceptions, even those scholars who are aware of the language-specific character of the 'mind concept' [...] seem convinced that the implicit Anglocentrism is benign". But is it really? Can we use the cultural constructs of one language, no matter how prevalent it is, to deconstruct those of another? Such deconstructions may look convincing to those who are fully conversant with the cultural constructs relied on. To others, in particular those whose cultural constructs are being deconstructed in this way, they do *not* look convincing and are likely not to mean anything at all. For native speakers of English, it may be hard to imagine what is wrong with descriptions of *duša* in terms of "the Russian soul", to give but one example. Readers in this category are invited to pause for a few seconds and ponder how they would feel about descriptions of *soul* as "the English *duša*". They do seem to lack cognitive plausibility, right? Well, so do the aforementioned descriptions of *duša* in terms of "the Russian soul". We cannot use words like *mind* and *soul* to capture authentic "insider perspectives" on EPCs (or any other concepts, for that matter) in other languages.

Many will argue that this places us in an impossible bind. No matter how hard we try, we are always going to be bound by the limitations placed upon us by the language in which we think. Or are we?

3 The NSM Approach

This book is aimed at those who are prepared to envisage the possibility that we do not need to remain "imprisoned in English" (Wierzbicka, 2014). There is an alternative: "Wierzbicka's prison metaphor implies that the possibility of escape exists – as it does from any other prison – but that this requires conscious effort, creativity, and planning" (Levisen, 2018: 3). The alternative is known as the "NSM approach", and it is presented in more detail in this section (for a recent, significantly more ambitious overview, see Goddard, 2018).

3.1 Primes and Explications

NSM is a powerful descriptive tool consisting of a maximally culture-neutral vocabulary and syntax developed over the last several decades by Anna Wierzbicka and Cliff Goddard, who, apart from relying on their own investigations, have been able to put to the best possible use the painstaking research carried out by linguists in Australia and elsewhere on dozens of typologically and genetically unrelated languages from all corners of the world. The NSM *approach*, which is inspired by a desire to overcome ethnocentrism and in particular Anglo bias in linguistic analysis, is the paradigm in linguistic semantics that uses NSM in its endeavour to *explicate* (i.e. make explicit) the meaning of culture-specific words and phrases using a technique known as 'reductive paraphrase'. This technique aims at *reducing* and ultimately removing cultural complexity by re-*paraphrasing* it into semantically simple terms. The result is referred to as an *explication*. Explications are fine-grained and, above all, non-Anglo-based descriptions that the English language as such is woefully inadequate to emulate in ways that are convincing to native speakers of other languages. Written in nontechnical language, they are accessible to cultural insiders (those for whom English is their native language) and cultural outsiders (all others) alike. The NSM approach has been illustrated in hundreds of publications, details of which are available on https://nsm-approach.net, a fully searchable and continually updated online database of relevant bibliographic notices.

NSM vocabulary is in essence limited to 65 so-called *semantic primes*. The list is now considered near-final. The primes are concepts or building blocks that are found in all (or nearly all) of the world's languages and that NSM practitioners believe to be semantically irreducible. They have resisted all attempts at semantic decomposition into more basic elements and are therefore deemed indefinable in terms that are semantically simpler than the primes themselves. NSM syntax is as universal as the primes, it is empirically validated, and it sets the rules for the combination of primes into the semantic components that make up an explication. Each of the primes has its own set of combinatorial properties. Since, until compelling evidence to the contrary (or unless stated otherwise; cf. Section 3.3), nothing in an explication is non-universal, explications can be translated without deformation or bias into other languages (other NSMs), thereby making culturally specific terms universally intelligible.

The English exponents of the primes, grouped into meaningful categories, are listed in Appendix B. Comparable tables for many other languages, as well as charts that summarize the combinatorial properties of the various primes, can be found on the NSM homepage at http://bit.ly/1XUoRRV.

3.2 *"Every explication is an experiment"*

NSM has been used extensively to prove how a culture-neutral and language-independent tool relying on a set of empirically grounded and universally applicable semantic primes, such as I, YOU, SAY, WANT, FEEL, THINK, KNOW, GOOD, and BAD, can help us see through the complex meanings of culture-specific concepts such as EPCs. But NSM was not always what it is today; it has come a long way since its first incursions into the field of ethnopsychology, which coincide more or less with the creation of the term *NSM* itself. Some early primes have been abandoned, and many more have been added. The combinatorial properties of primes have been clarified. Explications have been subjected to a constant process of further elaboration and fine-tuning. New tools have been added to the NSM toolkit, including but not limited to semantic molecules (Section 3.3) and semantic templates (Section 3.4).

For NSM practitioners, no explication is ever final – or, to put it differently, "every explication is an experiment" (Cliff Goddard).[4] To illustrate this motto, let us look at the consecutive developmental stages of the explication of one particular EPC, the one that has perhaps exercised the minds (*sic!*) of NSM practitioners more than any other: namely *mind*. I will not say everything that could possibly be said about the various stages in terms of the primes that are used and the grammar that holds them together as this would lead us too far away from the topic at hand. Instead, I will focus on the differences from one stage to the next.

A first attempt at explicating *mind* (Wierzbicka, 1989: 49) is reproduced in [A].[5]

[A]

(a)   one of the two parts of a person

(b)   one cannot see it

(c)   because of this part, a person can think and know

Explication [A] depicts the mind as the invisible counterpart to the body, which is not mentioned (for reasons that will become clear); it is the part that enables us to acquire knowledge and to engage in all sorts of intellectual processes. However, instead of the kind of technical jargon exemplified in this paragraph, the explication uses words that are cross-translatable and universally intelligible: *cannot see* instead of *invisible*, *because of* instead of *enable*, *think* instead of *engage in intellectual processes*, *know* instead of *acquire knowledge.* The explication is slightly revised three years later (Wierzbicka, 1992: 45):

[B] *mind*

(a) one of two parts of a person

(b) one cannot see it

(c) because of this part, a person can think and know

A caption has been added (the use of captions was not standard from the beginning), and the definite article in component (a) has gone missing ('one of the two parts' > 'one of two parts'). The removal of the article is not as inconsequential as it looks: it reflects the idea that the mind is thought of as complementary to the body without ruling out other dichotomies, such as "body and soul". The definite article in explication [A] precluded that possibility.

Explication [C] (Goddard & Wierzbicka, 1995: 46) has an expanded component (b):

[C] *mind*

(a) one of two parts of a person

(b) people cannot see it; people cannot touch it

(c) because of this part, a person can think

(d) because of this part, a person can know things

The reference to people's inability to touch the mind is a one-off. The new prime PEOPLE is used in component (b) instead of the pronoun *one*. This is an improvement since 'one' in 'one cannot see it' (explications [A] and [B]) is not an instance of the prime ONE, which is used in component (a). Thinking and knowing are separated out over two components to avoid the use of 'and', which is not a prime either. A direct object, 'things', is added in component (d) but not in component (c).

For the next attempt, we have to wait until the mid-2000s (Wierzbicka, 2005: 270):

[D] *The English "mind"*

(a) one of two parts of a person

(b) people cannot see this part

(c) because of this part, a person can think about things

(d) because of this part, a person can know things

The 'it' in component (b) is replaced with an explicit noun phrase ('this part'), referring to the numeral 'one' in component (a). The reference to untouchability is removed. 'Think' in component (c) now also gets a complement, which is prepositional ('about things'). Explications [E], [F], and [G] are all Goddard's. They are explicitly based on Wierzbicka's earlier work. [E] is from Goddard (2007: 25).

[E] *mind* (a person's *mind*)

(a) one of two parts of someone (one part is the body, this is the other part)

(b) people cannot see this part

(c) because someone has this part, this someone can think about things

(d) because someone has this part, this someone can know things

(e) when someone thinks about something, something happens in this part

There are several important differences between explications [D] and [E]. The change from 'a person' to 'someone' in component (a) follows the dismissal of the former as a so-called allolex of the prime SOMEONE. Allolexes are word forms that express a single meaning in complementary contexts. They are an important feature in the NSM lexicon that can be further exemplified by means of the complementarity between I and ME, or between THIS and THESE, etc. From now on, the prime retains only one form, which is used even in contexts where the former allolex was the preferred option until now (e.g. after a determiner: THIS PERSON > THIS SOMEONE). The change reflects the realization that the word *person* refers to a concept that is not semantically simple and introduces unnecessary culture-specificity into the explication. Its presence in the caption is tolerated.

Still in component (a), the identity of the two 'parts of someone' is further specified. Never before had the prime BODY made its appearance in explications of the word *mind*. The English word *body* has different meanings in the phrases *body and mind* and *the head and the body* (roughly, BODY without the head). The meaning associated with the prime is that of the former of the two phrases. Goddard and Peeters (2006: 18) point out that BODY was elevated to prime status (and therefore no longer deemed to be decomposable) in Goddard (2001a), but it is in fact already mentioned in earlier work: in Wierzbicka (1998), it appears for the first time in a table of primes and is used in a few semantic explications.[6] No *compelling* evidence has been found since that time that questions the status of BODY as a semantic prime (Wierzbicka, 2014: 40–51).

The 'because of' formulation in components (c) and (d) of explication [D] is replaced with a full-fledged clause ('because someone has this part'). Component (e) is new. It is a reference to the dynamic aspect of the *mind* concept, for which there exists linguistic evidence (cf. expressions such as *What's going on in his mind?* or phrases such as *the workings of the mind*).

Between [E] and [F] (Goddard, 2008: 79), the changes are minimal. The caption expands, triggering a change in component (a), where the prime THIS is added in front of the prime SOMEONE.

[F] someone's *mind* (a person's *mind*)

(a) one of two parts of this someone (one part is the body, this is the other part)

(b) people cannot see this part

(c) because someone has this part, this someone can think about things

(d) because someone has this part, this someone can know things

(e) when someone thinks about something, something happens in this part

[G] (Goddard, 2010: 83) heralds a return to a simpler caption; this time, the phrase between brackets is removed. Note the use of 'people' in components (c) and (d), as opposed to 'someone' in [E] and [F]. The plural form will not be maintained after 2010.

[G] someone's *mind*

(a) one of two parts of this someone (one part is the body, this is the other part)

(b) people cannot see this part

(c) because people have this part, people can think about things

(d) because people have this part, people can know things

(e) when someone thinks about something, something happens in this part

Levisen and Jogie (2015: 179) are the first to list components in clusters instead of one by one. Their explication is reproduced in [H].

[H] Anglo English *mind*

(a) something

    this something is one of two parts of someone

    one part is the body, this is the other part

    people cannot see this part

(b) because someone has this part, this someone can think about many things

    at the same time, because someone has this part, this someone can know many things

(c) when someone thinks about something, something happens in this part

There is no *someone* in the caption, which means there is no demonstrative with the prime SOMEONE in (mega)component (a). The old component (a) in [G] is pulled apart. For the first time, the mind is referred to as "something". The new (mega)component (a) (four lines) also refers to the mind's invisibility. The remaining three components of [G] are spread out over (mega)components (b) and (c). In (b), the quantifier MANY is added as the trigger for the plural 'things', which is an allolex of SOMETHING.

Wierzbicka (2016: 458) compares explication [I], which follows one year later, to her first attempts (explications [A] and [B]), noting that "in the course of the intervening two decades, both the lexicon and the syntax of the natural semantic metalanguage have been perfected" but that the "references to two parts of a person and to thinking and knowing" have been preserved.

[I] someone's *mind*

(a) something

(b) this something is part of this someone

(c) people cannot see this something

(d) this something is not part of this someone's body

(e) when this someone is thinking about something, something happens in this part

(f) because this someone has this part, it is like this:

(g)   this someone can think many things about many things

(h)   this someone can know many things about many things

The "reference to two parts of a person" is not as clear as Wierzbicka makes out since component (b) could imply that there are more than two parts to someone in any given conceptualization, not just the body and the mind. Another novelty is the assertion that, while the mind is part of someone (component (b)), it is not a body part (component (d)). The dynamic aspect gets promoted (i.e. moves higher up) and now precedes the references to thinking and knowing, which are grouped together in a subordinate scenario introduced by 'it is like this' (rather than being linked together with 'at the same time'). In addition, the thinking and knowing abilities are made syntactically equivalent: both verbs have a direct object and a prepositional complement, and the quantifier MANY is used to underscore that the mind is at the basis of a multitude of thoughts and knowledge.

Levisen (2017: 123) combines aspects of explications [H] and [I], and applies a "semantic template" specifically devised for EPCs (for more information, see Section 3.4). The template closely mirrors the (mega)components in explication [H]. The result appears in [J]:

[J] *mind* (someone's *mind*)

(a) something   GENERAL CONCEPTUAL STATUS

 this something is a part of this someone

 this part is not a part of the body

 people cannot see this part

(b) because someone has this part, it is like this: CHARACTERISTICS

  this someone can think about things

  this someone can know things

(c) when someone thinks about something,   DYNAMICS
 something happens in this part

This is how far NSM practitioners had come by the time this book went to press. It is more than conceivable, though, that we have not reached the end of the road and that, in light of new insights gained from the study of EPCs worldwide, more adjustments will be made as time goes on.[7]

3.3 Semantic Molecules

Thanks to its universal lexicon of primes and its universal grammar, NSM is quite unlike other metalanguages used in linguistics.

It is a mini-language, usually rendered in English but translatable into all other languages, that allows for explications to be framed without the burden of unnecessary associations with material from either the source or the target language. The tool is well suited to the analysis of EPCs as it enables us to make sense of what are often very culture-specific constructs with simple words and simple grammar rather than with potentially misleading vocabulary. Such misleading vocabulary could belong to the target language, i.e. the language of the analyst, the one used in the explications: we do not want references to the mind or the heart, and we want to avoid words such as *soul* and *spirit* since they would import all sorts of connotations that are foreign to the languaculture we are trying to better understand. For a genuine insider perspective, we need to work with words and/or concepts that make sense to the speakers of the source language. By the same token, material that belongs to the source language but cannot be rendered in the target language is equally unwanted. Cultural outsiders need to be able to understand our explications with the same ease as cultural insiders.

Sometimes, though, it just cannot be done with primes alone. Attempts to systematically exclude non-prime material may at times lead to very cumbersome explications that even a template structure such as the one illustrated at the end of the previous section would fail to render more palatable. Apart from primes, some explications may need to rely on so-called *semantic molecules*. To distinguish the latter from genuine primes, molecules are usually formally identified by a following lowercase *m* placed between square brackets, i.e. "[m]". Unlike primes, molecules are complex and not necessarily universal. However, they could still be widely shared across languages of the modern world. They are never posited lightly. Their main function is to maintain the overall readability of explications that would otherwise become impenetrable. Most importantly, they can and must be independently decomposed into semantic primes (or into combinations of primes and more basic molecules, as the case may be).

To give but one example, many languages, including English, have a soul-like construct that cannot be easily (or fully) explicated without reference, at least in passing, to a divine presence of some sort. To illustrate once more all the difference the use of a template can make, we reproduce in the following Levisen's (2017: 124) explication of the Russian concept *duša*, which he bases on work by Wierzbicka. *Duša* shares some of its features with English *soul* and *heart* but does not match either. As for the molecule *God*, used in the explication, Levisen does not identify it as such; we have added the "[m]" for him.

[K] *duša* **(someone's** *duša***)**

(a) something inside this someone   GENERAL CONCEPTUAL STATUS

   this something is a part of this someone

   the part is not a part of the body

   people cannot see this part

(b) because someone has this part, it is like this: CHARACTERISTICS

   this someone is not like other living things

   this someone can feel many things when this someone
   thinks about something

   this someone can be someone good

   (this someone can live with God [m])

(c) when something happens to someone,   DYNAMICS
   good things can happen in this part of someone

   when something happens to someone, bad things can happen in this part
   of someone

A recent explication of the molecule *God* appears in [L] (adapted from
Wierzbicka, 2015: 1084; for a different explication, see Habib, 2015):

[L] God

(a) someone not like people

   this someone is someone above people

   people cannot see this someone

   there is no one else like this someone

   God is this someone

(b) God is someone good

   if God wants something, it is something good

   if God says something, it is true

   if God wants something to happen, it can happen because of this

(c) God knows everything

God knows all people

God wants to do good things for all people

God feels something good toward all people

all people can know God, God wants this

It should be clear that any attempt to embed all the information contained in [L] into the explication of *duša* would severely compromise its readability. This, then, is how NSM practitioners proceed to keep their explications manageable. Semantic templates can play a similar role.

3.4 Semantic Templates

Semantic templates have been proposed not only for EPCs but also for several other lexical categories and for higher-order categories such as proverbs and metaphors. They provide a structure that captures shared aspects, thereby making comparison of explications both easier and more effective. The use of templates allows for a more focussed comparison: it makes more sense to compare components in meaningful clusters[8] than it does to go straight down to the smallest meaningful level, which is that of individual components.

Two templates have been proposed for EPCs so far.[9] Ideally, there should be only one; time will tell which one is better. Templates, like explications, are experiments (cf. Section 3.2). Levisen's (2017) template has already been exemplified in explications [J] and [K]; it has a tripartite structure (*General conceptual status*, *Characteristics*, and *Dynamics*) that can, however, be expanded.[10] Levisen (2017: 126) explains, in NSM, what each of the three blocks is about. The first block answers the question "what it is"; the second answers "what it is like"; and the third answers "what can happen because of this something", including "what can happen in this part", "what can happen to this part", "what it (sometimes) can be like", and "what it (sometimes) wants to do".

Wierzbicka's (2016) template, on the other hand, consists of four blocks; there is no suggestion that it could be expanded. Unlike Levisen's captions, Wierzbicka's are written in NSM, thus falling in line with the explication itself. The following is Wierzbicka's (2016: 469–470) explication of the New Testament Greek EPC ψυχή (*psyche*):

someone's *psykhe*

[A] [WHAT IT IS]
something inside this someone
this something is part of this someone
people cannot see this something
people cannot touch this something
this something is not part of this someone's body
this something is something very good

**[B] [HOW THIS SOMEONE CAN THINK ABOUT
THIS SOMETHING]**
this someone can think about this something like this:
  "this something is like someone
  this something can want something very much
  this something can feel something very bad,
      sometimes this something can feel something very good
  I can say something to this something"
at the same time this someone can think about this something like this:
  "this something is me"

[C] [WHAT THIS PART OF SOMEONE IS LIKE]
this part of someone is not like anything else
people have this part, (other) living things do not have a part like this
because of this, people are not like (other) living things

**[D] [WHAT PEOPLE CAN KNOW ABOUT THIS PART
OF SOMEONE]**
people can know that it is like this:
  after someone dies, this part of this someone does not die

because of this, after this someone dies, this someone can live in
another way

when this someone lives in this other way, this someone can live forever

at the same time, people can know that it is like this:

something very bad can happen to this part of someone,

if this happens, it is very bad for this someone

it can happen if this someone does something bad

other people cannot do anything bad to this part of someone

The use of NSM in captions is an innovation worthy of further exploration. Most templates that have been proposed over the years, including Levisen's, have relatively short captions that are printed in small capitals on the right-hand side of the first line of the blocks they name. This typographical layout, which is now well established, has the advantage of standing out and providing clear guidance to the overall structure of an explication as well as an indication of what each block contributes to the explication as a whole. This was another reason for the introduction of templates (in addition to their primary role of facilitating comparison, as explained earlier). Captioned templates are a useful device in the case of longer explications, which readers might otherwise find difficult to follow through to the end. They provide additional navigational help.

But the established typographical layout comes at a price: the brevity required to enable them to be printed on the right-hand side of an explication makes it impossible to use NSM, and captions that are not in NSM may be counterproductive as they go against the very spirit of NSM semantics. This is why, in recent work, Wierzbicka and one or two other authors rely on captions printed in big capitals at the top of their respective blocks, which goes against established practice but allows for the use of NSM, even in captions.

Overall, of the two templates that have been proposed for EPCs, Levisen's is in my view the most promising one; Section 4 explains why. The use of NSM to *comment* on captions (as opposed to formulating captions *in* NSM) may be a compromise solution we need to investigate further. This is not to say that there is no room for improvement to Levisen's template itself. It may well need to be further refined; at the instigation of the editor, but always using their own insights, two of the contributors to this volume make suggestions to this effect.

4 This Volume

Of the four contributions following this introduction, only the one by Yuko Asano-Cavanagh (who works on Japanese) does not explicitly rely on a semantic template. Her study has been placed first. The author complements earlier NSM work on *ki* 気 and *kokoro* 心 (Hasada, 2002; Svetanant, 2013) with a study on two EPCs on which there is hardly any literature, in spite of their importance in the Japanese languaculture. The two newly investigated EPCs are *inochi* 命 'life' and *tamashii* 魂 'soul'. The translations are at best approximate; Asano-Cavanagh points out that they are problematic, hence the need for more detailed explications.

The other three contributors either adopt or adapt a template that had been used before, or start from scratch. This is entirely coincidental. Contributors were not given any guidance as to how to frame their explications. It was left up to them, with a vague promise of some brainstorming sessions later on aimed at creating uniformity. The promise was not kept because the submissions that had come in were so wonderfully complementary that a decision was made to turn that complementarity into one of the defining features of the book and to order the contributions accordingly. Each of the submissions was externally peer-reviewed by at least two non-NSM scholars, who were told not to engage with the NSM explications if they did not feel so inclined. The editor, on the other hand, did liaise with individual authors on a number of NSM-related issues.

Thus, what we see here is an evolving NSM approach, one where each author, to the best of their ability, contributes to the field, being bound only by the requirement to use NSM, not by any guidelines as to *how* to use it.

Of course, the question, for those authors who decided to use a template, was how to figure out which template to use. Would it be one of their own making, and if so, what would be their guiding principle(s)? Or would it be one that had been used before, and if so, which one? And if it was to be one that had been used before, would they use it as is, or would they make changes to it, for whatever reason?

Deborah Hill, in her study on Longgu, an Oceanic language, adopts Wierzbicka's (2016) template for EPCs virtually as is, just making some minor amendments to the captions for blocks [C] and [D]. These are detailed in her chapter, which proposes a detailed explication for the Longgu EPC *anoa*, usually referred to in English as someone's 'spirit'. A person's *anoa* turns into an *agalo* when the individual dies, and another explication, using a very similar structure, is devised for *agalo* 'ancestor spirit'. Hill's chapter also provides explications for the Longgu concept *zabe* 'body and spirit' and for the place name Marapa, which is the nearby island where the *agalo* tend to congregate.

Chavalin Svetanant, in her study on Thai, casts new light on the evolution of the *chai* construct. Expanding on earlier work (Svetanant, 2013), she adds a fourth block to Levisen's (2017) tripartite template, which is unable to accommodate all the components she feels are necessary for an adequate explication of the Thai EPC *chai* ใจ 'heart'. Again, the gloss is at best approximate. Svetanant summarizes and exemplifies modern usage of the word, then retraces its history starting in the 13th century. She shows how *chai* conquers new territory over time, never losing its original meaning but piling up layers and layers of new, often metaphorical, uses. All that painstakingly collected information is then put to good use in the compilation of a detailed explication.

Colin Mackenzie, in his study on Old Norse-Icelandic, refers to the templates used by Wierzbicka (2016) and Levisen (2017) but ends up using his own, the first traces of which can be found in the PhD thesis on which his chapter builds. There is a striking difference in approach: whereas Wierzbicka and Levisen base their respective templates on years of engagement with EPC explications, Mackenzie, who works on an extinct language, builds on the intuition that diversity of EPCs in the world's languages, both current and extinct, is by no means limitless. Biological factors constrain the potential variety. As he puts it in earlier work, with reference to Gaby (2008: 39–40), "Our shared biological responses to stimuli provide the building blocks which cultures use to construct their emotional and psychological categories" (Mackenzie, 2014: 10). As human beings, we are capable of knowledge, thoughts, and feelings that we associate with one or more entities; these are cultural constructs but are nonetheless located somewhere in or around our bodies. Different capabilities can be linked up with different entities in culturally specific ways, although it could just as well be the case that a single entity is related to all. Finally, the entities usually engage in behaviours or are otherwise affected by the capabilities they are associated with. Each of these parameters of cultural, but biologically constrained variation is the focus of a different block in Mackenzie's template, which turns out to be not too different from Levisen's but was arrived at through an altogether different procedure. In my view, this is confirmation of the superiority of

Levisen's template or a variation on it. In his chapter, Mackenzie uses the template he comes up with to account for the meaning of the word *hugr* 'mind, heart, courage' in Old Norse-Icelandic. He also provides evidence of the difference NSM can make in all sorts of ways in the study of historical semantics, especially the historical semantics of EPCs.

5 Conclusion

Goddard (2008: 94) writes as follows:

> I would suggest that the presence in all languages and in all human conceptual systems of the concept BODY is partly responsible for the prevalence in languages of nominal expressions designating non-physical parts of a person, i.e., parts akin to the *heart, mind, soul*, and so on. Why? Because in a sense the semantic primes BODY and SOMEONE together pose a kind of conceptual problem: given that a person has a body, and given that there is evidently more to a person than a body alone – what else is there? Ethnopsychological constructs are answers to this question, and [...] a multiplicity of different answers (different cultural solutions) are provided in the languages and cultures of the world.

Taking our cue from Wierzbicka (2006: 166), we can formulate this in NSM as follows[11]:

(a) people in all places think about people like this:

   "all people have two parts

   people can see one of these two parts (the body)

   people cannot see the other part"

(b) when people think about this other part, they can think about it in many ways

   people in one place do not think about it like people in another place think about it

Efforts to show that there are scores of different EPCs in the languages of the world, and reminders that English words such as *heart, mind,* and *soul* cannot be used as universal yardsticks by means of which to describe the EPCs of other languages, need to continue to be widely relayed. The studies in this volume are one more step in this direction; they all use the same methodology, the same descriptive tool (NSM), so as to allow differences between the EPCs of various languacultures to be brought to the fore in a straightforward and illuminating way.

Appendix A

EPCs Explicated in NSM

Language (alphabetical)	EPC	Explicated in
Biblical Hebrew	*nepesh, khilyot-ay, lib-i*	Wierzbicka (2016)
Chinese	*xīn* 心	Kornacki (1995); Li, Ericsson, & Quennerstedt (2013)
Dalabon	*beng, kanûm*	Evans (2007)
Danish	*sind, sjæl, ånd*	Levisen (2012, 2017)
East Cree	*maamituneyihchikan, mituneyihchikan*	Junker (2003)
English	*mind, soul, heart*	Wierzbicka (1976, 1989, 1992, 2005, 2016); Goddard & Wierzbicka (1995); Goddard (2001b, 2003, 2007, 2008, 2010); Levisen & Jogie (2015); Levisen (2017)
Japanese	*kokoro* 心, *ki* 気, *mune* 胸, *hara* 腹, *seishin* 精神, *inochi* 命, *tamashii* 魂	Hasada (2002); Wierzbicka (1991, 2005); Svetanant (2013); Asano-Cavanagh (this volume)
Korean	*maum* 몸, *kasum* 가슴, *simcang* 심장	Yoon (2004, 2007, 2008); Wierzbicka (2005); Goddard (2007, 2010); Levisen (2017)
Latin	*anima*	Wierzbicka (2016)
Longgu	*anoa, agalo*	Hill (this volume)
Malay/ Indonesian	*hati*	Goddard (2001b, 2003, 2007, 2008); Gusmeldi (2017)
New Testament Greek	*psyche* ψυχη	Wierzbicka (2016)
Old English	*mōd*	Mackenzie (2014, this volume)
Old Norse-Icelandic	*hugr*	Mackenzie (2014, this volume)

(*Continued*)

Language (alphabetical)	EPC	Explicated in
Russian	*duša* душа, *serdce* сердце	Wierzbicka (1989, 1990, 1992, 2005); Goddard & Wierzbicka (1995, 2002); Goddard (2003); Gladkova (2013); Levisen (2017)
Thai	*chai* ใจ	Svetanant (2013, this volume)
Trini (creole)	*mine*	Levisen & Jogie (2015)
Yolngu	*birrimbirr*	Wierzbicka (2016)

Appendix B

Semantic Primes (English Exponents), Grouped into Related Categories

I, YOU, SOMEONE, SOMETHING~THING, PEOPLE, BODY	substantives
KIND, PART	relational substantives
THIS, THE SAME, OTHER~ELSE	determiners
ONE, TWO, SOME, ALL, MUCH~MANY, LITTLE~FEW	quantifiers
GOOD, BAD	evaluators
BIG, SMALL	descriptors
KNOW, THINK, WANT, DON'T WANT, FEEL, SEE, HEAR	mental predicates
SAY, WORDS, TRUE	speech
DO, HAPPEN, MOVE	actions, events, movement
BE (SOMEWHERE), THERE IS, BE (SOMEONE/SOMETHING)	location, existence, specification
(IS) MINE	possession
LIVE, DIE	life and death
WHEN~TIME, NOW, BEFORE, AFTER, A LONG TIME, A SHORT TIME, FOR SOME TIME, MOMENT	time
WHERE~PLACE, HERE, ABOVE, BELOW, FAR, NEAR, SIDE, INSIDE, TOUCH	locational
NOT, MAYBE, CAN, BECAUSE, IF	logical concepts
VERY, MORE	augmentor, intensifier
LIKE~AS	similarity

Notes: Exponents of primes can be polysemous, i.e. they can have other, additional meanings. Exponents of primes may be words, bound morphemes, or phrasemes. They can be formally, i.e., morphologically, complex. They can have combinatorial variants or allolexes (indicated with ~). Each prime has well-specified syntactic (combinatorial) properties.

Notes

1 Goddard (2008: 94) describes it as "a concept that is semantically complex and exquisitely culture-bound".
2 The reference provided by Wierzbicka is incorrect: two 1985 papers by Schieffelin appear to have been mixed up.
3 See, for instance, Ameka & Breedveld (2004: 173), Peeters (2007: 90), Levisen (2012: 233), Ye (2017: 17), Wierzbicka (2018: 29).
4 The phrase pops up at just about every NSM workshop, and in many NSM-inspired talks and seminars, but to the best of my knowledge, Goddard has never used it in print.
5 The bracketed letters preceding components in all the explications, except [H] and [J], are absent from the source documents. They have been added for easier cross-reference in the comments that follow.
6 In some ways, these explications are reminiscent of formulations in Wierzbicka (1988) and in the work it is based on, but in that earlier work 'body' was still considered to be a "near-primitive" (Wierzbicka 1985: 9) at best: it was thought to be semantically complex and therefore not a semantic prime in the true sense of the word. Its use in semantic explications was condoned for practical reasons. Wierzbicka's early work (e.g. 1975: 509, 1980: 169–170) provides semantic explications of the English word *body* that have never been explicitly dismissed as inadequate but obviously are. They date from about the same period as Brown's (1976) and Andersen's (1978) useful surveys of body-part nomenclature, in which the meaning 'body' is claimed to be universally lexicalized.
7 The careful reader will have noticed the disappearance of the quantifier MANY, resulting in a lack of clarity as to what triggers the plural 'things' in the part called *Characteristics*.
8 As far as I can see, there is no agreed-upon terminology for the "parts of a template"; in this volume, the term *block* is used, rather than *part* or *section*, to avoid potential confusion with the prime PART(S) and with the subdivisions, often called *sections*, found in most academic papers.
9 The template used by Svetanant (2013) is based on unpublished proposals that eventually led to one of them. It is not included in the count.
10 In some cases, there is a need for a *Social valuation* block that might contain statements such as 'it is good if other people can know what happens in this part of someone' (Levisen, 2017: 125) or 'it is good if people can think with this part at all times' (*ibid.*: 131).
11 Our formulation differs from Wierzbicka's in just one way: it avoids referring to 'a person' in the second line of part (a) and replaces this reference with one to 'all people' instead. This is in line with the latest developments in NSM (see Section 3.2). Some typographical layout improvements have been applied as well.

References

Ameka, Felix K., & Breedveld, Anneke (2004). Areal cultural scripts for social interaction in West African communities. *Intercultural Pragmatics, 1*(2), 167–187. doi:10.1515/iprg.2004.1.2.167
Andersen, Elaine S (1978). Lexical universals of body-part terminology. In Joseph H. Greenberg (Ed.), *Universals of human language: Vol. 3.*

26   *Bert Peeters*

Word structure (pp. 335–368). Stanford, CA: Stanford University Press.

Brown, Cecil H (1976). General principles of human anatomical partonomy and speculations on the growth of partonomic nomenclature. *American Ethnologist, 3*(3), 400–424. doi:10.1525/ae.1976.3.3.02a00020

Evans, Nicholas (2007). Standing up your mind: Remembering in Dalabon. In Mengistu Amberber (Ed.), *The language of memory in a crosslinguistic perspective* (pp. 67–95). Amsterdam: John Benjamins. doi:10.1075/hcp.21.06eva

Gaby, Alice (2008). Gut feelings: Locating intellect, emotion and life force in the Thaayorre body. In Farzad Sharifian, René Dirven, Ning Yu, & Susanne Niemeier (Eds.), *Culture, body, and language: Conceptualizations of internal body organs across cultures and languages* (pp. 27–44). Berlin: Mouton de Gruyter. doi:10.1515/9783110199109.2.27

Gladkova, Anna (2013). 'Intimate' talk in Russian: Human relationships and folk psychotherapy. *Australian Journal of Linguistics, 33*(3), 322–343. doi:10.1080/07268602.2013.846453

Goddard, Cliff (2001a). Lexico-semantic universals: A critical overview. *Linguistic Typology, 5*(1), 1–65. doi:10.1515/lity.5.1.1

Goddard, Cliff (2001b). *Hati*: A key word in the Malay vocabulary of emotion. In Jean Harkins & Anna Wierzbicka (Eds.), *Emotions in crosslinguistic perspective* (pp. 171–200). Berlin: Mouton de Gruyter. doi:10.1515/9783110880168.167

Goddard, Cliff (2003). Thinking across languages and cultures: Six dimensions of variation. *Cognitive Linguistics, 14*(2/3), 109–140. doi:10.1515/cogl.2003.005

Goddard, Cliff (2007). A culture-neutral metalanguage for mental state concepts. In Andrea C. Schalley & Drew Khlentzos (Eds.), *Mental states: Vol. 2. Language and cognitive structure* (pp. 11–34). Amsterdam: John Benjamins. doi:10.1075/slcs.93.04god

Goddard, Cliff (2008). Contrastive semantics and cultural psychology: English *heart* vs. Malay *hati*. In Farzad Sharifian, René Dirven, Ning Yu, & Susanne Niemeier (Eds.), *Culture, body, and language: Conceptualizations of internal body organs across cultures and languages* (pp. 75–102). Berlin: Mouton de Gruyter. doi:10.1515/978311019 9109.2.75

Goddard, Cliff (2010). Universals and variation in the lexicon of mental state concepts. In Barbara Malt & Phil Wolff (Eds.), *Words and the mind: How words capture human experience* (pp. 72–92). Oxford: Oxford University Press. doi:10.1093/acprof:oso/9780195311129.003.0005

Goddard, Cliff (2015). Words as carriers of cultural meaning. In John R. Taylor (Ed.), *The Oxford handbook of the word* (pp. 380–398). Oxford: Oxford University Press. doi:10.1093/oxfordhb/9780199641604.013.027

Goddard, Cliff (2018). *Ten lectures on Natural Semantic Metalanguage: Exploring language, thought and culture using simple, translatable words.* Leiden: Brill. doi:10.1163/9789004357723

Goddard, Cliff, & Peeters, Bert (2006). The Natural Semantic Metalanguage (NSM) approach: An overview with reference to the most important Romance languages. In Bert Peeters (Ed.), *Semantic primes and universal grammar: Evidence from the Romance languages* (pp. 13–38). Amsterdam: John Benjamins. doi:10.1075/slcs.81.07god

Goddard, Cliff, & Wierzbicka, Anna (1995). Key words, culture and cognition. *Philosophica, 55*(1), 37–67.

Goddard, Cliff, & Wierzbicka, Anna (2002). Semantics and cognition. In Lynn Nadel (Ed.), *Encyclopedia of cognitive science* (pp. 1096–1102). New York: John Wiley.

Gusmeldi, Ridha Fitryani (2017). *Indonesian cultural keyword* hati *and its English translation.* Master's thesis, Australian National University.

Habib, Sandy (2015). Can *God* and *Allah* promote intercultural communication? *RASK International Journal of Language and Communication, 42*, 77–103.

Harré, Rom (1998). *The singular self: An introduction to the psychology of personhood.* London: Sage.

Hasada, Rie (2002). 'Body part' terms and emotion in Japanese. *Pragmatics and Cognition, 10*(1), 107–128. doi:10.1075/pc.10.12.06has

Hayes, Cecilia (2018). *Cognitive gadgets: The cultural evolution of thinking.* Cambridge, MA: Harvard University Press.

Junker, Marie-Odile (2003). A native American view of the "mind" as seen in the lexicon of cognition in East Cree. *Cognitive Linguistics, 14*(2/3), 167–194. doi:10.1515/cogl.2003.007

Kornacki, Paweł (1995). *Heart & face: Semantics of Chinese emotion concepts.* PhD thesis, Australian National University.

Levisen, Carsten (2012). *Cultural semantics and social cognition: A case study on the Danish universe of meaning.* Berlin: de Gruyter Mouton. doi:10.1515/9783110294651

Levisen, Carsten (2017). Personhood constructs in language and thought: New evidence from Danish. In Zhengdao Ye (Ed.), *The semantics of nouns* (pp. 120–146). Oxford: Oxford University Press. doi:10.1093/oso/9780198736721.003.0005

Levisen, Carsten (2018). Biases we live by: Anglocentrism in linguistics and cognitive sciences. *Language Sciences* (in press, corrected proof). doi:10.1016/j.langsci.2018.05.010

Levisen, Carsten, & Jogie, Melissa Reshma (2015). The Trinidadian 'theory of mind': Personhood and postcolonial semantics. *International Journal of Language and Culture, 2*(2), 169–193. doi:10.1075/ijolc.2.2.02lev

Li, Jing, Ericsson, Christer, & Quennerstedt, Mikael (2013). The meaning of the Chinese cultural keyword *xin*. *Journal of Languages and Culture, 4*(5), 75–89. doi:10.5897/JLC12.054

Mackenzie, Colin Peter (2014). *Vernacular psychologies in Old Norse-Icelandic and Old English.* PhD thesis, University of Glasgow.

Palmquist, Stephen R. (Ed.) (2010). *Cultivating personhood: Kant and Asian philosophy.* Berlin: Mouton de Gruyter.

28   *Bert Peeters*

Peeters, Bert (2007). Australian perceptions of the weekend: Evidence from collocations and elsewhere. In Paul Skandera (Ed.), *Phraseology and culture in English* (pp. 79–107). Berlin: Mouton de Gruyter. doi:10.1515/9783110197860.79

Schieffelin, Edward (1985). The cultural analysis of depressive affect: An example from New Guinea. In Arthur Kleinman & Byron Good (Eds.), *Culture and depression: Studies in the anthropology and cross-cultural psychiatry of affect and disorder* (pp. 101–133). Berkeley, CA: University of California Press.

Scott, G. E. (1990). *Moral personhood: An essay in the philosophy of moral psychology.* Albany, NY: SUNY Press.

Sharifian, Farzad, Dirven, René, Yu, Ning, & Niemeier, Susanne (Eds.) (2008). *Culture, body, and language: Conceptualizations of internal body organs across cultures and languages.* Berlin: Mouton de Gruyter. doi:10.1515/9783110199109

Svetanant, Chavalin (2013). Exploring personhood constructs through language: Contrastive semantic of "heart" in Japanese and Thai. *The International Journal of Interdisciplinary Studies in Communication, 7*(3), 23–32.

Torchia, Joseph (2007). *Exploring personhood: An introduction to the philosophy of human nature.* Lanham, MD: Rowman & Littlefield.

Wierzbicka, Anna (1975). Why "kill" does not mean "cause to die": The semantics of action sentences. *Foundations of Language, 13*(4), 491–528.

Wierzbicka, Anna (1976). Mind and body. In James McCawley (Ed.), *Syntax and semantics: Vol. 7. Notes from the linguistic underground* (pp. 129–157). New York: Academic Press.

Wierzbicka, Anna (1980). *Lingua mentalis: The semantics of natural language.* Sydney: Academic Press.

Wierzbicka, Anna (1985). *Lexicography and conceptual analysis.* Ann Arbor, MI: Karoma.

Wierzbicka, Anna (1988). *The semantics of grammar.* Amsterdam: John Benjamins. doi:10.1075/slcs.18

Wierzbicka, Anna (1989). Soul and mind: Linguistic evidence for ethnopsychology and cultural history. *American Anthropologist, 91*(1), 41–58. doi:10.1525/aa.1989.91.1.02a00030

Wierzbicka, Anna (1990). *Duša* (soul), *toska* (yearning), *sud'ba* (fate): Three key concepts in Russian language and Russian culture. In Zygmunt Saloni (Ed.), *Metody formalne w opisie języków słowiańskich* (pp. 13–32). Bialystok: Bialystok University Press.

Wierzbicka, Anna (1991). Japanese key words and core cultural values. *Language in Society, 20*(3), 333–385. doi:10.1017/S0047404500016535

Wierzbicka, Anna (1992). *Semantics, culture, and cognition: Universal human concepts in culture-specific configurations.* Oxford: Oxford University Press.

Wierzbicka, Anna (1998). Russian emotional expression. *Ethos, 26*(4), 456–483. doi:10.1525/eth.1998.26.4.456

Wierzbicka, Anna (2005). Empirical universals of language as a basis for the study of other human universals and as a tool for exploring cross-cultural differences. *Ethos, 33*(2), 256–291. doi:10.1525/eth.2005.33.2.256

Wierzbicka, Anna (2006). On folk conceptions of mind, agency and morality. *Journal of Cognition and Culture, 6*(1/2), 165–179. doi:10.1163/156853706776931286

Wierzbicka, Anna (2014). *Imprisoned in English: The hazards of English as a default language.* New York: Oxford University Press. doi:10.1093/acprof:oso/9780199321490.001.0001

Wierzbicka, Anna (2015). Natural semantic metalanguage. In Karen Tracy, Cornelia Ilie, & Todd Sandel (Eds.), *The international encyclopedia of language and social interaction* (pp. 1076–1092). New York: John Wiley.

Wierzbicka, Anna (2016). Two levels of verbal communication, universal and culture-specific. In Andrea Rocci & Louis de Saussure (Eds.), *Verbal communication* (pp. 447–482). Berlin: Mouton de Gruyter. doi:10.1515/9783110255478-024

Wierzbicka, Anna (2018). Speaking about God in universal words, thinking about God outside English. In Paul Chilton & Monika Kopytowska (Eds.), *Religion, language, and the human mind* (pp. 19–51). Oxford: Oxford University Press. doi:10.1093/oso/9780190636647.003.0002

Ye, Zhengdao (2017). The semantics of nouns: A cross-linguistic and cross-domain perspective. In Zhengdao Ye (Ed.), *The semantics of nouns* (pp. 1–18). Oxford: Oxford University Press. doi:10.1093/oso/9780198736721.003.0001

Yoon, Kyung-Joo (2004). Korean *maum* vs. English *heart* and *mind*: Contrastive semantics of cultural concepts. In Christo Moskovsky (Ed.), *Proceedings of the 2003 Conference of the Australian Linguistic Society.* Retrieved from http://www.als.asn.au/proceedings/als2003.html

Yoon, Kyung-Joo (2007). Contrastive semantics of Korean 'maum' vs. English 'heart' and 'mind'. *The Journal of Studies in Language, 22*(3), 171–197. doi:10.18627/jslg.22.3.200702.171

Yoon, Kyung-Joo (2008). The Korean conceptualization of *heart*: An indigenous perspective. In Farzad Sharifian, René Dirven, Ning Yu, & Susanne Niemeier (Eds.), *Culture, body, and language: Conceptualizations of internal body organs across cultures and languages* (pp. 213–243). Berlin: Mouton de Gruyter. doi:10.1515/9783110199109.3.213

2 *Inochi* and *Tamashii*

Incursions into Japanese Ethnopsychology

Yuko Asano-Cavanagh

1 Introduction

Modern technology has developed humanoid robots, also known as androids, who behave very much like human beings. In big cities in Japan, androids working at the reception desks of department stores, banks, and hospitals are by no means an uncommon sight. In the Osaka region, they are even programmed to speak the Kansai dialect of Japanese, and they are therefore able to communicate with customers in a natural manner. Their facial expressions resemble those of human beings, so much so that it may at times be hard to distinguish between an android and a real person.

Naturally, humanoid robots do not experience sensations, thoughts, emotions, wishes, or desires. These are specific to humans (and, to a lesser extent, animals), who are capable of such sensations, thoughts, emotions, wishes, or desires, thanks to their minds, hearts, souls, and other such ethnopsychological personhood constructs (EPCs). Cross-linguistic analyses have revealed that these are culture-specific and by no means universal (Wierzbicka, 1992, 2005; Goddard, 2008). Thus, the meaning of the English word *mind* is not equivalent to that of Russian *duša* (душа) or Trinidad English *mind/mine* (Wierzbicka, 1992; Levisen & Jogie, 2015). Likewise, Japanese has several EPCs lacking equivalents in other languages. Some of these have been subjected to previous analysis. *Kokoro* 心 'heart', *ki* 気 'energy', *mune* 胸 'chest', and *hara* 腹 'belly' have all been examined and identified as EPCs governing Japanese people's emotions and mentality (Hasada, 2002; Ikegami, 2008; Occhi, 2008; Svetanant, 2013). They are perceived by speakers of Japanese as the invisible parts of a person by means of which that person can think and feel.

Two terms that, to the best of my knowledge, have not been described before, at least not with the same attention to detail, are the nonphysical *inochi* 命 and *tamashii* 魂, both of which are crucial to understanding the concept of existence from a Japanese cultural perspective. Both are indigenous Japanese lexemes. The term *inochi* is usually translated as 'life'. However, the modern English word *life* is polysemous, and the meaning of *inochi* is considerably narrower than that of the word *life* in English. *Tamashii* is often rendered as 'soul'. Even so, the contextual usage of the term strongly suggests that it has different connotations.

The chapter starts with a brief comparison of *life* and *inochi*, followed by an in-depth examination of the latter (Section 2). It then does the same for *soul* and *tamashii* (Section 3), which is in addition compared to *kokoro* 'heart'. It will be shown that *inochi* and *tamashii* both describe, albeit in different ways, the notions of being, existence, as well as life force, and that both, albeit to a different extent, refer not only to humans, but to plants, animals, and the physical environment as well. The demonstration will first and foremost rely on web-based examples of how Japanese speakers use the words *inochi* and *tamashii* in various situations.

2 Inochi 命

Whereas *kokoro* 'heart' and *ki* 'energy' are specific to human beings, *inochi* 命 extends to animals, plants, and other creatures as well. Without *inochi*, people, animals, plants, and other creatures are dead. According to Morioka (1991), the word *inochi* can be found in ancient Japanese literature, such as the *Manyōshū* and the *Kojiki*, which date back to the 8th century.

2.1 Life *and* Inochi 命: *A Quick Comparison*

Examples of its usage in Japanese suggest that *inochi* 命 represents something of significant importance. Learners of Japanese as a foreign language who are told that it translates as 'life' often face difficulties when trying to understand the exact meaning of the Japanese word and to use it in the correct context. Other translational 'equivalents', such as *vita* in Italian or *vie* in French, cause similar confusion.

The main issue here is the polysemous nature of terms such as *life*, *vita*, and *vie*. The following list of meanings of the English word was derived from information found in two online dictionaries

(*Cambridge*, https://dictionary.cambridge.org/dictionary/english/
life; *Merriam-Webster*, https://www.merriam-webster.com/dictionary/
life):

'the period between birth and death';

'the sequence of physical and mental experiences that make up
the existence of an individual';

'a way or manner of living';

'a particular part of someone's life';

'biography';

'the period of duration, usefulness, or popularity of something';

'the quality that makes people, animals, and plants different
from objects, substances, and things that are dead'.

Clearly, the English word *life* represents a wide variety of concepts.
We can only know the exact meaning of the word by examining
it within its context. On the other hand, *inochi* is typically used
among Japanese speakers 'when they refer to everyday phenomena
concerning life, death, and nature' (Morioka, 1991: 86). Examples
of *inochi* used in context suggest that the expression connotes something of immense importance and significance to the Japanese.
For instance, it is well known that former Prime Minister Takeo
Fukuda made the following comment when he decided to pay a
ransom to ensure the safety of the hostages on a Japan Airlines
flight hijacked in 1977 (Alexander, 2002: 346):

1   一人の命は全地球よりも重い。

*Hitori no **inochi** wa zen-chikyū yorimo omoi.*

'The weight of one person's *life* is greater than that of the entire
Earth' (lit. One person's *life* is heavier than the entire earth).

The Prime Minister's remark meant that the protection of the hostages' *inochi* ought to be regarded as a top priority, more important than anything else. However, the literal translation conveys a
different connotation to the actual meaning that 'there is nothing more precious than *inochi*'. The remark touched the hearts of
the Japanese and has been repeatedly quoted since the incident.

The following examples indicate how ordinary Japanese speakers prioritize *inochi* above all else:

2 タクシー運転手になって3年以上が経ちましたが、他人の命を預かっているという重みを日に感じます。

*Takushii-untenshu ni natte san-nen ijō ga tachimashita ga, tanin no **inochi** o azukatteiru to iu omomi o hi ni kanjimasu.*

'More than three years have passed since I became a taxi driver but I still feel the weight of the responsibility of having other peoples' *inochi* in my hands each and every day'.

(http://www.asahi.com/and_s/articles/7.html [2017])

3 安全運転。守るべきものは、何よりも命。

*Anzen-unten mamoru beki mono wa, naniyorimo **inochi**.*

'Safe driving. What I should be protecting above all else are *inochi*'.

(https://www.asahi.com/and_s/articles/13.html?iref=comtop_fbox_u07 [2017])

4 小さな命。みんなで守る。

*Chiisana **inochi** minna de mamoru.*

'Young *inochi*. We must all protect it'.

(http://www.asahi.com/articles/DA3S13119368.html [2017])

In these examples, drivers express the strong sense of responsibility they feel for their passengers' *inochi*. Translating this highly culture-specific Japanese word as 'life' fails to adequately convey how indispensable both the word and the concept are in the Japanese worldview.

2.2 *The Meaning of* Inochi 命

This section of the chapter is devoted to the explication of the meaning of the word *inochi* 命 using the semantic primes and molecules of the Natural Semantic Metalanguage (NSM).

First of all, *inochi* is like other EPCs, such as *kokoro* 'heart' or *mune* 'chest', in terms of its location (Hasada, 2002): a person's *inochi* is inside the body. A verb often used in that context, especially with reference to pregnancies, is the verb *yadoru* 宿る, which roughly means 'dwell', 'inhabit', or 'reside' (cf. Examples 5 and 6):

5 新しい命が宿った時の事について、インタビューしなければならないのですが。

*Atarashii **inochi** ga **yadotta** toki no koto ni tsuite, intabyū shi-nakerebanaranai no desu ga.*

'I will need to conduct an interview about the time when a new *inochi* came to *inhabit* (your body)'.

(https://oshiete.goo.ne.jp/qa/5568479.html [2010])

6 初めてお腹に新しい命が宿った時はどんな気持ちになったのでしょうか?

*Hajimete o-naka ni atarashii **inochi** ga **yadotta** toki wa donna kimochi ni natta no deshō ka?*

'How did it feel when you became pregnant for the first time?' (lit. How did you feel when a new *inochi* came to *inhabit* your womb for the first time?)

(https://detail.chiebukuro.yahoo.co.jp/qa/question_detail/q11178594416 [2017])

7 私が双子のお母さんに・・・願ってもいなかった幸運がやってきた。二つの命が、私に・・・。

*Watashi ga futago no o-kā-san ni…Negatte mo inakatta kōun ga yattekita. Futatsu no **inochi** ga, watashi ni…*

'I will be a mother of twins. A happiness I never dreamt of has come to me. Two *inochi* are inside of me'.

(https://akasugu.fcart.jp/taikenki/entry/2017/02/22/052025 [2017])

As suggested in Examples 5 and 6, the sequence "a new *inochi*" is routinely used to refer to an unborn baby growing inside the mother's womb. While it is there, *inochi* stays inside the baby. It follows that if a mother is expecting twins, as in Example 7, she has two babies' *inochi* inside her. *Inochi* becomes a part of the body from the moment of conception. This can be paraphrased as follows:

someone's *inochi* 命

something inside someone's body,

this something is a part of this someone's body

Next, similarly to *kokoro* 'heart', *mune* 'chest', and *ki* 'energy', *inochi* is invisible:

8 いのちは、目に見えない、手で触れないけれど、みんな持っています。周りにある空気も目に見えません。でも、空気がなければ生きていけません。いのちも空気も大切なものは目に見えないのです。

Inochi *wa, me ni mienai, te de furenai keredo, minna motteimasu. Mawari ni aru kūki mo me ni miemasen. Demo, kūki ga nakereba ikiteikemasen.* **Inochi** *mo kūki mo taisetsuna mono wa me ni mienai no desu.*

'*Inochi* are invisible. Although we cannot touch them, everyone has one. The air around us is also invisible, but we cannot live without air. Important things, such as *inochi* and air, are not visible'.

(http://www.yamagata-u.ac.jp/sho/principalsoffice25.html [2017])

Even surgery will fail to find someone's *inochi* within their body. It simply cannot be seen: the meaning of *inochi* contains the component 'people cannot see it'.

While *kokoro* 'heart', *mune* 'chest', and *ki* 'energy' are specific to human beings, *inochi* is vital to the existence not only of human beings but also of animals, fish, plants, and other creatures (Morioka, 1991). *Kokoro* denotes the mental and emotional faculties (Occhi, 2008), and therefore sounds odd if associated with the latter, whereas *inochi* can be used naturally in association with any living organisms. Thus, it is possible to talk about *ningen no* **inochi** 人間の命 'human beings' *inochi*', *neko no* **inochi** 猫の命 'cats' *inochi*', *mushi no* **inochi** 虫の命 'insects' *inochi*', *sakana no* **inochi** 魚の命 'fish's *inochi*', *shokubutsu no* **inochi** 植物の命 'plants' *inochi*', *ki no* **inochi** 木の命 'trees' *inochi*', etc. This aspect can be represented by means of the following component:

all people have this part

people cannot live if they do not have this part

at the same time, it is like this:

all animals [m] have this part, all creatures [m] have this part, all fish [m] have this part, all birds [m] have this part, all plants [m] have this part, all trees [m] have this part.

Next, there is strong agreement among the Japanese that *inochi* is a one-off (Morioka, 1991). There are countless examples where *inochi* collocates with *ichido-kiri* 一度きり 'only once', 'once and for all':

9   「一度きりの人生」
「一度きりの命」
そうは思っても、その人生が苦しくて仕方がないと生きる気力を失ってしまう。

'Ichido-kiri no jinsei'
*'Ichido-kiri no **inochi**'*
Sō wa omottemo, sono jinsei ga kurushikute shikata ga nai to ikiru kiryoku o ushinatteshimau.

'We only get one life time'
'This is our one and only *inochi*'
Even if we know this is true, when our lives contain too much pain or difficulties to overcome, we can end up losing the will to live'.

(https://ameblo.jp/kenkenpapa1217/entry-12295356801.html [2017])

10   なんのために生まれたのか、一度きりの命をどう輝かせるのか。

*Nan no tameni umareta no ka, ichido-kiri no **inochi** o dō kagay-akaseru no ka.*

'Why were we born? How can we make our one and only *inochi* shine?'

(https://www.crazy.co.jp/blog/articles/woman-careea-lifelanguage/ [2017])

11   人生の目的を教えてください。一度きりの命。思う存分、楽しむことさ！それ以外にない。

*Jinsei no mokuteki o oshietekudasai. – Ichido-kiri no **inochi**. Omou zonbun, tanoshimu koto sa! Sore igai ni nai.*

'Tell me the purpose of life. – The purpose is surely to fully enjoy our one and only *inochi*. There is nothing else'.

(https://detail.chiebukuro.yahoo.co.jp/qa/question_detail/q10171121745 [2017])

These examples clearly show that *inochi* can be inside a body only once. This can be phrased as follows: 'this something can be a part of someone one time, not many times'.

Inochi is limited in terms of its duration. If the body gets severely damaged due to old age, illness, or injury, *inochi* cannot be sustained, as indicated in Example 12:

12 私たちは命を持って生まれてきました。限りある命です。・・・誰にも命を
    終えるときがやってきます。・・・

    *Watashi-tachi wa **inochi** o motte umaretekimashita. Kagiri aru
    inochi desu…Dare nimo **inochi** o oeru toki ga yattekimasu…*

    'We are all born possessing *inochi*. *Inochi* that are limited …
    The time comes to everyone when their *inochi* will end…'.

    (https://ameblo.jp/kotoiroshi/entry-1i12288836673.html [2017])

As the end eventually comes for any *inochi*, people often talk in terms of 'saving *inochi*', 'losing *inochi*', or stress the importance of not 'devaluing *inochi*':

13 自分には命を助けることも、食べ物を届けることもできない。

    *Jibun niwa **inochi** o tasukeru koto mo, tabemono o todokeru koto
    mo dekinai.*

    'I am not even able to save *inochi* or deliver food'.

    (http://www.asahi.com/articles/ASK8N36Q5K8NTLZU006.html?iref=
    comtop_8_03 [2017])

14 津波で命を落とした仲間の遺志を受け継ぎ、ブランドパートナーとして
    結果を出したい。

    *Tsunami de **inochi** o otoshita nakama no ishi o uketsugi, burando-
    pātonā toshite kekka o dashitai.*

    'I would like to fulfil the last wishes of my friends and associates who lost their *inochi* in the tsunami, I would like to produce a result as their brand partner'.

    (http://www.nupalette.jp/archives/1539 [2017])

15 命を粗末にしたらダメだ。頑張って生きないと。

    ***Inochi** o somatsunishitara dame da. Ganbatte ikinai to.*

    'We cannot devalue *inochi*. We must strive to continue living' (lit. 'We cannot waste *inochi*/use *inochi* carelessly').

    (http://education.mag2.com/osusume/2008/07/135.html [2008])

Inochi is the part of the body that keeps the living organism alive. Similarly to English *life*, one cannot say that '*inochi* dies' (?'*Inochi ga shinu*'). It is when someone loses their *inochi* that they die. Accordingly, when *inochi* is separated from a body, it causes death. This aspect can be represented as follows:

if something very bad happens to someone's body, this something cannot be a part of this someone's body anymore

when something like this happens, this someone cannot live anymore

On the basis of what has been said, the meaning of *inochi* can now be explicated as follows:

someone's *inochi* 命

(a)   something inside someone's body

(b)   this something is a part of this someone's body

(c)   people cannot see this part

(d)   all people have this part

(e)   people cannot live if they do not have this part

(f)   at the same time, it is like this:

   all animals [m] have this part, all creatures [m] have this part, all fish [m] have this part, all birds [m] have this part, all plants [m] have this part, all trees [m] have this part

(g)   this something can be a part of someone one time, not many times

(h)   if something very bad happens to someone's body, this something cannot be a part of this someone's body anymore

(i)   when something like this happens, this someone cannot live anymore

The explication relies on a number of semantic molecules that may, in some cases, interfere with its direct translatability into other languages but that are necessary to convey the fact that, in the eyes of the Japanese, *inochi* are not a mere human attribute. However, as a human attribute, they are vital to the human existence, in spite of their nonphysicality. *Inochi* are invisible, but no one can deny their reality.

3 *Tamashii* 魂

Although, in contemporary written Japanese, it is six to seven times less frequently used than *inochi*,[1] *tamashii* 魂, too, is a word that reveals a lot about the Japanese perspective on existence. It seems to be a derivative of *tama*, a much older word (but not as old as *inochi*) that can be found, for instance, in the work of the 14th-century writer Kenkō Yoshida (Kindaichi, 2014). The meaning of the word has not drastically changed since that time. Why it was eventually replaced with *tamashii* in modern Japanese is up for debate. One possible explanation is the need to distinguish it from another word *tama* 玉 meaning 'ball' or 'bundle'.

3.1 Soul *and* Tamashii 魂 *Compared*

Tamashii 魂 is usually translated into English as 'soul': for instance in the 2003 *Kenkyusha New Japanese-English Dictionary*. In much the same way as references to the soul are far less common in English nowadays than they used to be (Wierzbicka, 1992: chapter 1), people in modern Japanese culture are not nearly as likely to talk about their *tamashii* as they are about their *inochi*. This may be due to the fact that the word *tamashii*, like its English counterpart (if that is what it is), represents an elusive concept that not everyone believes in. No Japanese will question the fact that every human being, when alive, has an *inochi*, but some do question the reality of *tamashii*, as in Example 16:

16 人間に魂はあるか。魂がないのなら人間と物質との違いは何か。

Ningen ni **tamashii** *wa aru ka.* **Tamashii** *ga nai no nara ningen to busshitsu no chigai wa nani ka.*

'I wonder if human beings have *tamashii*. If not, how do they differ from non-living things?'

(https://detail.chiebukuro.yahoo.co.jp/qa/question_detail/q11114240326 [2013])

Such existential doubts, which could never be raised with reference to people's *inochi* (??*Ningen ni* **inochi** *wa aru ka* 'I wonder if human beings have *inochi*'), can be challenged by those who do not harbour them:

17 魂や霊を信じない方は、何を根拠に信じないんですか?

Tamashii *ya rei o shinjinai kata wa, nani o konkyo ni shinjinai n desu ka?*

'To those who do not believe in *tamashii* or spirit, on what basis do you not believe?'

(https://detail.chiebukuro.yahoo.co.jp/qa/question_detail/q1171021696 [2011])

One of the reasons, if not the only reason, why the concept behind the word *soul* is so elusive is probably that it is tied up with a number of religious and spiritual concepts, making it difficult for some to believe in what it stands for. The soul belongs to a spiritual world based on Christian traditions, in which it is linked to one or more immaterial good beings (such as God and his angels). It has a transcendental aspect and possesses an 'other-worldly' nature, as well as a moral character that ties in with the idea of being good (Wierzbicka, 1992: 35–39). The soul is thought to be "the source of values in a human being" (*ibid.*: 36).[2]

What about *tamashii*? There is no indication of *tamashii* having dual aspects of being 'good' or 'bad'. In addition, *tamashii* does not possess or suggest 'other-worldliness'. It is simply a part of human beings who are alive in the material world. Above all, however, *tamashii*, unlike *soul*, is linked to ideas of reincarnation, and, like *inochi*, it can be an attribute not only of human beings but also of animals as well as plants (but not of insects and fish, for instance).

3.2 Tamashii 魂 *versus* Kokoro 心

Several scholars, including Hasada (2002), Ikegami (2008), Occhi (2008), and Svetanant (2013), have discussed the semantics of *kokoro* 心 'heart' in detail; Hasada and Svetanant have done so using NSM. Hasada (2002) claims the meaning of *kokoro* overlaps with that of both *mind* and *heart*; her explication, brought in line with current NSM practice, appears in the editor's postscript, together with a comment on Svetanant's revisions. None of these scholarly works touch on the relationship between *kokoro* 心 and *tamashii* 魂, which may be due to the fact that the question is far from clear. Some dictionaries state that *tamashii* "governs" *kokoro*, others declare *kokoro* a synonym of *tamashii*, and others still do both. Confusion also reigns among Japanese speakers, as demonstrated by Examples 18 and 19:

18   魂と心の違いを教えてください。

Tamashii to kokoro no chigai o oshietekudasai.

'Could you tell me the difference between *tamashii* and *kokoro*?'

(https://detail.chiebukuro.yahoo.co.jp/qa/question_detail/q1388051968 [2012])

19   「魂」と「心」とは何が違うのでしょうか。宗教や哲学によって考え方
は様々だと思うので回答者様が考える二つの違い（または同じ部分）
を参考意見と聞かせてください。

'Tamashii' to 'kokoro' to wa nani ga chigau no deshō ka. Shūkyō ya tetsugaku ni yotte kangae-kata wa samazama da to omou node kaitōsha-sama ga kangaeru futatsu no chigai (matawa onaji bubun) o sankō-iken to kikasetekudasai.

'What are the differences between *tamashii* and *kokoro*? I think the answer varies depending on one's religion or philosophy. So please let me know your opinion on the differences and similarities between them'.

(https://oshiete.goo.ne.jp/qa/4400114.html [2008])

The confusion is presumably caused by the fact that there are contexts where *tamashii* and *kokoro* can be used interchangeably. Consider Examples 20–22:

20   あなたの魂を揺さぶる、一曲は何ですか?

*Anata no **tamashii** o yusaburu, ik-kyoku wa nan desu ka?*

'Which song moves your *tamashii* deeply?'

(https://detail.chiebukuro.yahoo.co.jp/qa/question_detail/q11143898086 [2015])

21   女性の魂を奪うシャネルとルイ・ヴィトン。

*Josei no **tamashii** o ubau shaneru to rui-viton*

'Chanel and Louis Vuitton captivate women's *tamashii*'.

(http://blog.goo.ne.jp/yamansi-satoyama/e/9d56357a7130cc65a5285f26fdc4bc17 [2014])

22   魂が震えるほど惹きつけられる異性に出会ったことはありますか?

***Tamashii** ga furueu hodo hikitsukerareru isei ni deatta koto wa arimasu ka?*

'Have you ever met a member of the opposite sex that made your *tamashii* tremble?'

(https://detail.chiebukuro.yahoo.co.jp/qa/question_detail/q1081648440 [2012])

In Examples 20–22, *tamashii* can be replaced by *kokoro*, as illustrated in Examples 23–25:

23   あなたの心を揺さぶる、一曲は何ですか?

   *Anata no **kokoro** o yusaburu, ik-kyoku wa nan desu ka?*

   'Which song moves your *kokoro* deeply?'

24   女性の心を奪うシヤネルとルイ・ヴィトン。

   *Josei no **kokoro** o ubau shaneru to rui-viton*

   'Chanel and Louis Vuitton captivate women's *kokoro*'.

25   心が震えるほど惹きつけられる異性に出会ったことはありますか?

   ***Kokoro** ga furueru hodo hikitsukerareru isei ni deatta koto wa arimasu ka?*

   'Have you ever met a member of the opposite sex that made your *kokoro* tremble?'

Interchangeability does not mean equivalence of meaning, though. The connotations of both sets of sentences are not the same. The sentences containing *tamashii* somehow sound as if the person's whole body is involved, whereas the sentences containing *kokoro* indicate that only a part of the person (namely, their *kokoro* 'heart') has been affected.

   In other contexts, *tamashii* is inappropriate and only *kokoro* can be used. *Tamashii* cannot replace *kokoro* in Examples 26–28:

26   被災地での演奏「逃げ出したい」。心を変えた言葉 。

   *Hisaichi de no ensō 'nigedashitai'. **Kokoro** o kaeta kotoba.*

   'I felt like running away from the musical concert organized at the disaster area. But someone's words changed my *kokoro*'.

   (http://www.asahi.com/articles/ASK8N36Q5K8NTLZU006.html?iref=comtop_8_03 [2017])

27   彼女がいるのに心が揺れている自分に自己嫌悪しています。

   *Kanojo ga iru noni **kokoro** ga yureteiru jibun ni jiko-keno shiteimasu.*

   'I hate myself because my *kokoro* has become uncertain about my girlfriend'.

   (https://oshiete.goo.ne.jp/qa/8994553.html [2015])

28 次々にこうした喪失体験に向き合っていく老年期は、心が非常に不安
定になりやすい年代なのです。

*Tsugitsugini kōshita sōshitsu-taiken ni mukiatteiku rōnen-ki wa,
kokoro ga hijōni fuanteini nariyasui nendai na no desu.*

'People's *kokoro* become very unstable in old age when they are
faced with experiencing the loss of one person after another'.

(https://this.kiji.is/279537232209477636 [2017])

Someone's words may change one's *kokoro* but not one's *tamashii*
(Example 26). *Kokoro*, but not *tamashii*, can be plagued by uncer-
tainty (Example 27) and become unstable in old age (Example 28).
This suggests that *kokoro* can be affected by cognitive as well as
emotional experiences: it can alter its stance or state by feeling *and
also by thinking*, whereas *tamashii* cannot. Unlike *kokoro*, *tamashii*
is not a place where people can conceive or process thoughts.[3]
   To further illustrate this point, consider Examples 29 and 30,
where *tamashii* would sound extremely odd:

29 あらゆる環境においても心が狭い人は必ず存在します。

*Arayuru kankyō ni oite mo **kokoro** ga semai hito wa kanarazu
sonzaishimasu.*

'People with narrow *kokoro* exist in any environment'.

(https://mayonez.jp/topic/7562 [2017])

30 心の広い人···それは他人に対して寛容で自分とは異なった考え方や意
見を許容できる人のことです。

***Kokoro** no hiroi hito… Sore wa tanin ni taishite kanyōde jibun to
wa kotonatta kangae-kata ya iken o kyoyōdekiru hito no koto desu.*

'People with wide *kokoro*… They are people who are tolerant
towards other people and who can accept different ways of
thinking or opinions different from their own'.

(http://www.mori-life.com/self/son-toku.htm [2017])

Kokoro ga hiroi 心が広い can be translated as 'broad-minded',
'open-minded', or 'big-hearted', and *kokoro ga semai* 心が狭い as
'narrow-minded'. As the English translations show, *kokoro* is the
place where people think (cf. *mind* in English). *Kokoro* can think
good things and bad things; it can think many things at the same
time, thereby growing or shrinking in size – becoming bigger or

smaller, or becoming wider or narrower. *Tamashii* sounds very unnatural in these kinds of contexts. *Tamashii* cannot change its state, shape, or condition; it cannot be said to be narrow or wide, big or small. This is presumably because *tamashii* does not process someone's thinking, whereas *kokoro* does.

3.3 The Meaning of Tamashii 魂

As we saw in the previous two sections, *tamashii* 魂 is semantically close (but by no means identical) to *soul*, yet at the same time there are similarities with *kokoro* as well. There is a clear need to conduct a rigorous semantic analysis of the word *tamashii*, aimed at uncovering the differences between its meaning and that of closely associated EPCs in Japanese and other languages. The following is a first step in that direction. Once again, real-life examples will be allowed to speak for themselves and will guide us towards an explication that will hopefully inspire others to do similar work leading to further improvements.

Before we bring *kokoro* back into the picture, let us look at what *tamashii* shares with *inochi*. First, similar to *inochi*, *tamashii* is inside a person's body. Once again, the verb that is used is *yadoru* 宿る. People often say *tamashii* 'dwell in' or 'inhabit' (*yadoru*) the bodies of human beings:

31   魂が存在するとして、人に魂が宿るのはいつからでしょうか？

*Tamashii ga sonzaisuru toshite, hito ni **tamashii** ga **yadoru** no wa itsu kara deshō ka?*

'Assuming that *tamashii* exist, from what point do *tamashii* inhabit human beings?'

(http://q.hatena.ne.jp/1159454807 [2006])

Tamashii are inside the human body, thus making them a part of human beings, but no one knows exactly where they are located. They are not tangible, and, as attested by Examples 27 and 28, they cannot be seen either:

32   大切なものは目に見えません。命、魂、空気、気、意識、心、思い、愛な
　　 どは目に見えませんが、確かに存在します。

*Taisetsuna mono wa me ni miemasen. Inochi, **tamashii**, kūki, ki, ishiki, kokoro, omoi, ai nado wa me ni miemasen ga, tashikani sonzaishimasu.*

'Things of importance are invisible. *Inochi* 'life', *tamashii* 'soul', air, *ki* 'energy', consciousness, *kokoro* 'heart', thoughts and feelings as well as love are invisible, but they all exist'.

(https://plaza.rakuten.co.jp/tajin/10001/ [2017])

33 なぜ人は、目に見えないものを信じることがあるのでしょうか？魂や、天
    国、地獄な・・・

    Naze hito wa, me ni mienai mono o shinjiru koto ga aru no deshō
    *ka? **Tamashii** ya, tengoku, jigoku nado...*

    'How can people believe in something that is invisible? *Tamashii*,
    heaven or hell....'

    (https://detail.chiebukuro.yahoo.co.jp/qa/question_detail/q1255561207 [2011])

Tamashii is thus an immaterial entity with a meaning that resembles and intertwines with some aspects of the meaning of *inochi*. It is suggested the first part of the explication of *tamashii* runs as follows:

someone's *tamashii* 魂

something inside someone's body

this something is a part of this someone

this something is not a part of this someone's body

people cannot see this part

The next question is whether *tamashii* can exist within any form of life.[4] It is possible to refer to *inu no **tamashii*** 犬の魂 'dogs' *tamashii*', *neko no **tamashii*** 猫の魂 'cats' *tamashii*', etc. A Japanese proverb has it that *issun no mushi nimo go-bu no **tamashii*** 一寸の虫にも五分の 魂, literally 'even in a small insect, a fifth is its *tamashii*', hence 'even the weakest and smallest of beings has its own will and therefore has significance'. In addition, at least some trees (especially those that are old and big) are said to have *tamashii*; it is unknown whether all trees have one. A tree's *tamashii* sometimes goes by a special name, *kodama* 木霊, and some people, because they believe in *tamashii* or *kodama*, would hesitate to cut down a tree:

34 洋風の家を建てたいため、松をかわいそうですが伐採することを考え
    ております。その際気になるのが「木には魂が宿る」という話です。で
    も木の魂といいますが、それは木によって魂があったりなかったり・・・

というのはどういうことなのでしょうか？樹齢が長いとか、大木・・・だと魂があって、鉢植えの木なら魂はないですか？

*Yōfū no ie o tatetai tame, matsu o kawaisō desu ga bassaisuru koto o kangaeteorimasu. Sono sai ki ni naru no ga 'ki ni wa **tamashii** ga yadoru' to iu hanashi desu. Demo ki no **tamashii** to iimasu ga, sore wa ki niyotte **tamashii** ga attari nakattari ... to iu no wa dōiu koto na no deshō ka? Jurei ga nagai toka, taiboku ... da to **tamashii** ga atte, hachiue no ki nara **tamashii** wa nai desu ka?*

'We would like to build a Western-style house, which would require cutting down the pine tree, however we feel sorry for the tree. What we are concerned about is whether or not "*tamashii* inhabit the tree". But when you say "a tree has *tamashii*", does that mean, some trees have *tamashii*, but some do not? If a tree is big or has lived many years, would the tree have *tamashii*, but a potted tree would not?'

(https://detail.chiebukuro.yahoo.co.jp/qa/question_detail/q12159239642 [2016])

On the other hand, it would be very odd to refer to the *tamashii* of flowers or fish. Thus, we cannot assume that all life forms have *tamashii*; on the other hand, according to the (sizeable) minority that denies their existence altogether, those life forms that many consider to have *tamashii* do not have *tamashii* either. The fact is that no one has ever either proved or disproved the reality of *tamashii*. However, according to mainstream Japanese ideology, it is implausible to claim that human beings, animals, and big trees *do not* have *tamashii*. The latter is thus something *many* Japanese people believe exists. This can be explicated as follows:

many, not all, people think like this:

    people have this part

at the same time, many, not all, people think like this:

    animals [m] have this part, a big tree [m] can have this part

Tamashii, for those who believe in it, can experience feelings, such as 'excitement', 'enchantment', 'fascination', or 'attraction', just as *kokoro* 'heart' can. This was illustrated in Section 3.2 by means of Examples 20–25. What does this mean for "the common view that *kokoro* is the seat of Japanese emotions" (Hasada, 2002: 111), a view the author translates into NSM by saying that 'because [someone] has this part, [this someone] can feel many things'?⁵ Would *tamashii* enjoy a similar status? It probably does not. It seems safer to describe *tamashii* in the following terms:

this something can feel many things

because of this, people can feel these things

they can feel these things inside this something

Hasada (2002: 111) also posits a component relating to thoughts: 'because [someone] has this part, [this someone] can think some things'. This is legitimate in the case of *kokoro*, but there is no corresponding component where *tamashii* is concerned. Indeed, Examples 26–28 (also in Section 3.2) illustrate that *kokoro*, but not *tamashii*, is associated with feelings *and* thoughts. *Tamashii* thus has a component 'this something can feel many things', but it does not have the component 'this something can think some things'.

Examples 35–38 illustrate yet another aspect of the meaning of *tamashii*:

35 肉体から魂が抜ける瞬間が撮影された。

*Nikutai kara **tamashii** ga nukeru shunkan ga satsueisareta.*

'The photo was taken at the very moment the *tamashii* left the body'.

(http://www.excite.co.jp/News/entertainment_g/20160720/Myjitsu_007822. html [2016])

36 魂と体が離れる感覚ってありますか?

***Tamashii** to karada ga hanareru kankaku tte arimasu ka?*

'Are you experiencing the sensation that your *tamashii* has left your body?'

(https://detail.chiebukuro.yahoo.co.jp/qa/question_detail/q1499561909 [2013])

37 人が住まなくなった家はすぐに傷むと言います。それと同様に、人の肉体は魂を宿すための「器」であり「入れ物」だから、魂が抜けかけた体はどんどんボロボロになってしまうのだと理解したのです。

*Hito ga sumanakunatta ie wa suguni itamu to iimasu. Sore to dōyōni, hito no nikutai wa **tamashii** o yadosu tame no 'utsuwa'*

*deari 'iremono' dakara, **tamashii** ga nukekaketa karada wa
dondon boroboro ni natteshimau no da to rikaishita no desu.*

'People say a house deteriorates if no one lives there. Likewise,
our body is a 'vessel' or a 'container' in which a *tamashii* lives.
So I understood that a body whose *tamashii* is separating also
deteriorates (falls apart)'.

(https://matome.naver.jp/odai/2147551264823418501 [2016])

38 父もそうでしたが、亡くなった方の顔を見ると人間から魂が離れたら、
本当にただの殻が残っているんだなあ、今回も強く感じました。空っぽ
の体はとても小さくて、しわなどもすべてなくなったような感じです。魂が
身体から離れて、次の旅へ出発した、とその空っぽの体を見ているとよ
くわかります。

*Chichi mo sō deshita ga, nakunatta kata no kao o miruto ningen
kara **tamashii** ga hanaretara, hontōni tadano nakigara ga nokotteiru
n da nā, konkai mo tsuyoku kanjimashita. Karappo no karada wa
totemo chiisakute, shiwa nado mo subete nakunatta yōna kanji
desu. **Tamashii** ga karada kara hanarete, tsugi no tabi he shuppat-
sushita, to sono karappo no karada o miteiru to yoku wakarimasu.*

'It was the same when my father passed away. Every time I have
seen a dead person's face, I have strongly felt that only a shell
remains after the *tamashii* has left the body. The empty body
seems small and the wrinkles seem to have disappeared. It is
obvious when I look at an empty body: the *tamashii* has de-
parted from the body to start on its next journey'.

(https://blogs.yahoo.co.jp/ulrikayui/7478067.html [2006])

The examples show that *tamashii* are considered to have a free will
to go anywhere if they wish to do so. In other words, *tamashii* can
separate from the body and therefore can be temporarily absent
from the body. It is very natural to say that a *tamashii* leaves one's
body, whereas *kokoro* and *inochi* cannot be used in these situations.
The examples also indicate that *tamashii* continue to be alive even
when they are out of the body. It is unclear, though, whether they
can actually leave one's body *whenever* they wish. Some people believe that *tamashii* can be absent from one's body when the person
is asleep. *Yūtai-ridatsu* 幽体離脱 'out-of-body experience' is a term
that refers to a state during which *tamashii* is temporarily separated
from a person's body while that person is asleep. On the other hand,
some people believe that *tamashii* stays in one's body throughout one's entire lifetime. There is no way to prove this either way.

Therefore, it is not plausible to claim that *tamashii* can go anywhere anytime if they wish. However, no one would deny that *tamashii* leave the body at the time of death. They can be inside one's body only while one is alive. When a person dies, their *tamashii* becomes separated from the body and gains its freedom. This can be stated as follows:

when someone dies, this something cannot be inside this someone's body anymore

after this someone dies, this something can go to any place at any time

The question then arises what happens to someone's *tamashii* after their death. In essence, for those who believe in them, *tamashii* are eternal by nature (like souls) and hence continue to exist indefinitely. In other words, *tamashii* are defined as immortal. Some authors (Umehara, 1992; Tagami, 2010) link *tamashii* to reincarnation, a fundamental concept of Buddhism (Woerner & Schuhmacher, 1994; Tagami, 2010). Since Japanese culture has been greatly influenced by the religious traditions of Shintoism, Buddhism, and Taoism (Ellwood & Pilgrim, 1992; Reader & Tanabe, 1998), it is no surprise that the meaning of *tamashii* should reflect an idea that came from these teachings and that is totally foreign to teachings about the soul. The claim that a *tamashii* can come back to a person's body many times and is reborn every time it enters the body of a new baby is reflected in examples of the word used in context, examples that reflect a common belief and that refer, for instance, to '*tamashii* that have been born many times' (*nando mo umarekawattekuru **tamashii***) and '*tamashii* that have been reborn very few times' (*umarekawatta kaisū ga sukunai **tamashii***).[6] *Inochi* cannot replace *tamashii* here. One can only talk naturally about a *tamashii* that reincarnates.

Another way of illustrating this is by observing that, where it is often said that *inochi* are *ichido-kiri* 'only once', 'once and for all' (cf. Section 2.2), the same cannot be said about *tamashii*. [?]*Ichido-kiri no **tamashii*** 'one and only *tamashii*' sounds odd, which corroborates the Japanese belief that *tamashii* can have many lives and exist indefinitely. Example 39 further illustrates this point:

39 魂は永遠ですが、この生涯は一度きり。誰に遠慮することなく、堂々と のびのびと、限られた命を活かしきりたいものですね。

Tamashii *wa eien desu ga, kono shōgai wa ichido-kiri. Dare ni enryosuru koto naku, dōdōto nobinobito, kagirareta **inochi** o ikashikiritai mono desu ne.*

'Although a *tamashii* is eternal, this life is only once. Do you not think we should make use of our limited *inochi* by living in a dignified but carefree manner without holding back?'

(https://ameblo.jp/kazunemisaki/entry-11825769953.html [2014])

Talk about *kagirareta* **tamashii** 限られた魂 'limited *tamashii*' is problematic, to say the least. As shown in Example 39, many Japanese speakers believe that *tamashii* continue to exist without limitation, whereas *inochi* are limited. Furthermore, since they can occupy a new baby's body, *tamashii* can experience numerous lives and therefore possess memories. This is one of the significant differences with English *soul*. Consider Examples 40 and 41:

40 魂の記憶が蘇ってくると、今までの人生の全てが、生まれるまえに魂が決めた計画どおりに、寸分の狂いもなく、進んできたことを思い出すことができます。

Tamashii *no kioku ga yomigaettekuru to, ima made no jinsei no subete ga, umareru mae ni* **tamashii** *ga kimeta keikaku-dōri ni, sunbun no kurui mo naku, susundekita koto o omoidasu koto ga dekimasu.*

'When the memories of your *tamashii* come back, you realize that everything in your life to date has proceeded precisely as your *tamashii* planned before you were born'.

(http://www.yamatofuji.com/blog/2011/04/post-188.html [2011])

41 大切なご縁も宇宙のしくみも自分のミッションもすべては魂の奥底に記憶されています。「私も、魂の記憶を呼び覚ませるような活動をしていきたい！」

Taisetsuna go-en mo uchū no shikumi mo jibun no misshon mo subete wa **tamashii** *no oku-soko ni kiokusareteimasu. 'Watashi mo,* **tamashii** *no kioku o yobisamaseru yōna katsudou o shiteikitai!'*

'Important ties and relationships, the nature of the universe and one's own mission in life are all recorded at the core of our *tamashii*. "I would like to continue working towards awakening the memories of peoples' *tamashii*!"'

(https://ameblo.jp/lily-wisteria/entry-12237870213.html [2017])

On the other hand, as *tamashii* can repeatedly enter new bodies, they naturally accumulate countless experiences and can age, i.e. move from new, or young, to old, as shown in Examples 42 and 43:

42   魂にも年齢があって、古い魂や新しい魂がある。

> **Tamashii** *ni mo nenrei ga atte, furui* **tamashii** *ya atarashii* **tamashii** *ga aru.*

'*Tamashii* can age. There are old *tamashii* and new *tamashii*'.

(https://www.gamitaka.com/soul-age.html [2015])

43   世の中には、まるで大人のような子供が時々います。人は生まれたときは みな同じだという人がいますが、そうではありません。若い魂もいれば、 年老いた魂もいます。世の中に彼らは混在しています。

> *Yononaka niwa, marude otona no yōna kodomo ga tokidoki imasu. Hito wa umareta toki wa mina onaji da to iu hito ga imasu ga, sō dewaarimasen. Wakai* **tamashii** *mo ireba, toshi-oita* **tamashii** *mo imasu. Yononaka ni karera wa konzaishiteimasu.*

'There are sometimes children who are like adults. Some people say we are all equal when we are born, but that's not the case. There are young *tamashii* and old *tamashii*. They live together in this world'.

(http://hidejin1221.wixsite.com/hidejin-notes/singlepost/2016/12/30/魂って何だ ろう？3 [2016])

Describing someone's *tamashii* as 'old' means that this person's *tamashii* has had many previous lives, which is different from what is meant by the expression *an old soul* in English. While it would not be natural to talk about [??]*a young soul*, a 'young *tamashii*' is a reference to one who does not have many past lives. On the other hand, as is often said, with age comes wisdom. References to 'wise' or 'omniscient' *tamashii* are not uncommon in Japanese. *Tamashii wa shitteiru* 'Omniscient *tamashii*' is the title of a 2008 book by author Miki Takasaka.

   To sum up, although people cannot deny the existence of *inochi*, some do reject the claim that *tamashii* exist. This is presumably because the concept itself implies reincarnation: *tamashii* can come back many times, each time entering the body of a new baby (human being or animal), gaining more experience, and becoming wiser. Nothing of this can be proved or measured scientifically, which is undoubtedly the very reason why the idea of *tamashii* is sometimes rejected. On the basis of these observations, the following new semantic components of *tamashii* can be formulated:

this something can be inside another baby's [m] body after this

this can happen many times

because of this, this something can be a part of someone many times

because of this, this something can know many things

Finally, although one can 'lose one's *inochi*' (***inochi** o otosu* 命を落とす), one cannot 'lose one's *tamashii*' (***tamashii** o otosu?*? 魂を落とす). It can be said that 'someone is trying to take *inochi*' (i.e. kill someone: ***inochi** o nerawareru* 命を狙われる), but not that 'someone is trying to take *tamashii*' (***tamashii** o nerawareru?*? 魂を狙われる). Similarly, an *inochi* ends one day, but a *tamashii* has no ending:

44   誰にも命を終えるときがやってきます。

*Dare ni mo **inochi** o oeru toki ga yattekimasu.*

'Everyone eventually ends their *inochi*'.

45   *??*誰にも魂を終えるときがやってきます。

*??Dare ni mo **tamashii** o oeru toki ga yattekimasu.*

Likewise, someone who was rescued from under the rubble of a collapsed home can talk about 'the person who saved my *inochi*' (命の恩人 ***inochi** no on-jin*), but a similar phrase with the word *tamashii* is impossible. These examples support the claim that *tamashii* are eternal: they cannot be hurt, injured, or damaged. *Tamashii* are immortal. This can be expressed as follows: 'this something cannot die'.

The full meaning of *tamashii* can now be explicated as follows:

someone's *tamashii* 魂

(a)   something inside someone's body

(b)   this something is a part of this someone

(c)   this something is not a part of this someone's body

(d)   people cannot see this part

(e)   many, not all, people think like this: people have this part

(f)   at the same time, many, not all, people think like this:

      animals [m] have this part, a big tree [m] can have this part

(g)   this something can feel many things

(h)   because of this, people can feel these things

(i)   they can feel these things inside this something

(j)   when someone dies, this something cannot be inside this person's body anymore

(k)   after this someone dies, this something can go to any place at any time

(l)   this something can be inside another baby's [m] body after this

(m)   this can happen many times

(n)   because of this, this something can be a part of someone many times

(o)   because of this, this something can know many things

(p)   this something cannot die

4 Conclusion

No one would deny that a human being or animal has a body as the body is something that is physically visible. One can see it, touch it, feel it. However, the existence of *inochi* 命 and *tamashii* 魂 is difficult to prove. In fact, there is no way in which to plausibly and scientifically prove or disprove their existence. However, although we cannot see a person's *inochi*, Japanese speakers do not doubt its existence. *Inochi* is a vital concept that distinguishes a live body from a dead one. Its meaning is fundamentally linked to the body's impermanence.

On the other hand, *tamashii* are equally invisible, but there is no specific life event, such as birth or death, that Japanese speakers can refer to as a point when it comes into or goes out of existence. Therefore, some Japanese people do not believe *tamashii* exist. However, not having scientific evidence of its existence gives us an important clue to its meaning. There are countless examples that suggest that the characteristics of *tamashii* link to a belief in reincarnation: the idea that, after death, a person's *tamashii* returns to life in another body. The belief in the immortality of *tamashii* presumably comes from Buddhist ideology. Although it is not possible to unequivocally prove the exact connection between the meaning of the word *tamashii* and the religious ideologies of Buddhism, linguistic evidence strongly suggests that the way the word is understood by the Japanese has been profoundly influenced by Buddhist teachings and ideologies. This is one of several significant differences between *tamashii*, on the one hand, and English *soul*, Russian *duša*, or Italian *anima* (Wierzbicka, 1992; Farese, in preparation), on the other. *Tamashii* is not only permanent but may also continually return to the lives of human beings and even to the lives of animals or big trees.[7]

The meanings of *inochi* and *tamashii* have been transmitted down through generations of speakers of the Japanese language and are thus culturally specific. The two words and the phrases they can enter into clearly reflect how Japanese people perceive their existence and relation to other animals, creatures, parts of the natural world including trees, as well as how they think about life and death.

Acknowledgements

I would like to express my gratitude to Bert Peeters for his detailed comments on an earlier draft of this chapter. I am also grateful to the anonymous reviewers for their comments. In addition, I would like to thank Elizabeth Miller for assistance in editing the text.

Editor's Postscript: Explication of *Kokoro* 心 'Heart' According to Hasada (2002)

To allow readers to undertake their own comparison of *tamashii* 魂 and *kokoro* 心, Hasada's (2002) explication of the latter, referred to by Yuko Asano-Cavanagh, is reproduced below, with a few adjustments reflecting recent advances in NSM methodology.

someone's *kokoro* 心

(a)   something inside someone's body

(b)   this something is a part of this someone

(c)   this something is inside the upper [m] part of the body

(d)   people cannot see it

(e)   because someone has this part, this someone can feel many things

(f)   someone can feel many kinds of things in this part,

(g)   not all kinds of things

(h)   because someone has this part, this someone can want to do some things

(i)   because someone has this part, this someone can think some things

(j)   because someone has this part, this someone can want to know what other people feel

(k)   someone can do good things for other people because of this

(l)   if someone does not have this part, this someone cannot be a good person

(m)   other people cannot know what happens in this part

Like all other NSM explications, Hasada's was an experiment, no matter how groundbreaking it was at the time. There is definitely room for improvement. An additional step, not envisaged in Asano-Cavanagh's chapter either, is the use of a semantic template. As pointed out in Peeters (this volume), different templates are used in each of the chapters that follow. A predecessor to one of them appears in Svetanant (2013), whose revision of Hasada's earlier explication is of interest in that it reveals aspects (such as an EPC's dynamics) that have tended to remain underdeveloped. Unfortunately, it uses some semantic primes that were abandoned a long time ago, thus making the updated version of Hasada's explication a better starting point for a fruitful comparison between *tamashii* and *kokoro*.

Notes

1   The *Balanced Corpus of Contemporary Written Japanese* (BCCWJ), which covers a wide range of text registers including books, newspaper articles, government white papers, magazines, school textbooks, internet bulletin boards, and blogs (Maekawa, Yamazaki, Ogiso et al., 2014), was consulted in its online 'Shonagon' version at http://www.kotonoha.gr.jp/shonagon/ to get a better feel of the frequency of both words. For the period 1976–2005, 20,050 tokens of *inochi* were found, compared to a mere 2950 of *tamashii*.

2   The word *soul* does have secondary meanings that are not relevant here. Cf. the definitions provided by Oxford Living Dictionaries (https://en.oxforddictionaries.com/definition/soul):

1   The spiritual or immaterial part of a human being or animal, regarded as immortal.
     a   A person's moral or emotional nature or sense of identity.
2   Emotional or intellectual energy or intensity, especially as revealed in a work of art or an artistic performance.
3   The essence or embodiment of a specified quality.
     a   An individual person.
     b   A person regarded with affection or pity.

3 It is possible to say *tamashii o ire-kaeru*, which literally means 'replace one's tamashii'. The phrase means 'to reform oneself', or 'to turn over a new leaf', and suggests not so much a shift in emotional state, but an overhaul resulting from a thought process that acts on it from the outside.

4 Some people believe that *tamashii* can reside in large rocks as well.

5 Corrections to the NSM are indicated in square brackets and reflect revisions to NSM implemented in more recent times.

6 https://ameblo.jp/tokumorikeiko/entry-11286353029.html [2012].

7 Interestingly, the meaning of *soul* might be currently undergoing a semantic shift from the original meaning due to influences from other religious teachings caused by globalization and the increased use of social media. A survey result showed that 22% of Christians in the USA believe in reincarnation (Pew Research Center, 2009), and therefore their interpretation of *soul* would be different from the original meaning and it would be closer to that of *tamashii*. Consequently, English speakers may have different understandings of its meaning, depending on their beliefs and backgrounds. In this way, the soul is a more elusive concept than ever.

References

Alexander, Yonah (Ed.) (2002). *Combating terrorism: Strategies of ten countries*. Ann Arbor, MI: University of Michigan Press. doi:10.3998/mpub.11969

Ellwood, Robert S., & Pilgrim, Richard (1992). *Japanese religion: A cultural perspective*. Englewood Cliffs, NJ: Prentice Hall.

Farese, Gian Marco (in preparation). The semantic journey of *anima* from Latin to Italian.

Goddard, Cliff (2008). Contrastive semantics and cultural psychology: English *heart* vs. Malay *hati*. In Farzad Sharifian, René Dirven, Ning Yu, & Susanne Niemeier (Eds.), *Culture, body, and language: Conceptualizations of internal body organs across cultures and languages* (pp. 75–102). Berlin: Mouton de Gruyter. doi:10.1515/9783110199109.2.75

Hasada, Rie (2002). 'Body part' terms and emotion in Japanese. *Pragmatics and Cognition, 10*(1), 107–128. doi:10.1075/pc.10.12.06has

Ikegami, Yoshihiko (2008). The heart: What it means to the Japanese speakers. In Farzad Sharifian, René Dirven, Ning Yu, & Susanne Niemeier (Eds.), *Culture, body, and language: Conceptualizations of internal body organs across cultures and languages* (pp. 169–190). Berlin: Mouton de Gruyter. doi:10.1515/9783110199109.3.169

Levisen, Carsten, & Jogie, Melissa Reshma (2015). The Trinidadian 'theory of mind': Personhood and postcolonial semantics. *International Journal of Language and Culture, 2*(2), 169–193. doi:10.1075/ijolc.2.2.02lev

Maekawa, Kikuo, Yamazaki, Makoto, Ogiso, Toshinobu, et al. (2014). Balanced corpus of contemporary written Japanese. *Language Resources and Evaluation, 48*(2), 345–371. doi:10.1007/s10579-013-9261-0

Morioka, Masahiro (1991). The concept of *inochi*: A philosophical perspective on the study of life. *Nichibunken Japan Review, 2,* 83–115. doi:10.15055/00000400

Occhi, Debra J. (2008). How to have a HEART in Japanese. In Farzad Sharifian, René Dirven, Ning Yu, & Susanne Niemeier (Eds.), *Culture, body, and language: Conceptualizations of internal body organs across cultures and languages* (pp. 191–212). Berlin: Mouton de Gruyter. doi:10.1515/9783110199109.3.191

Pew Research Center (2009). Reading the stars. Retrieved from http://www.pewresearch.org/fact-tank/2009/12/29/reading-the-stars/

Reader, Ian, & Tanabe, George J. (1998). *Practically religious: Worldly benefits and the common religion of Japan.* Honolulu, HI: University of Hawaii Press.

Svetanant, Chavalin (2013). Exploring personhood constructs through language: Contrastive semantic of "heart" in Japanese and Thai. *The International Journal of Interdisciplinary Studies in Communication, 7*(3), 23–32.

Tagami, Taishū (2010). *Butten no kotoba [Buddhist words].* Tokyo: Kodansha.

Takasaka, Miki (2008). *Tamashii wa shitteiru.* Tokyo: Gentō-sha.

Umehara, Takeshi (1992). *Nihonjin no tamashii [Japanese people's soul].* Tokyo: Kōbunsha.

Wierzbicka, Anna (1992). *Semantics, culture, and cognition: Universal human concepts in culture-specific configurations.* New York: Oxford University Press.

Wierzbicka, Anna (2005). Empirical universals of language as a basis for the study of other human universals and as a tool for exploring cross-cultural differences. *Ethos, 33*(2), 256–291. doi:10.1525/eth.2005.33.2.256

Woerner, Gert, & Schuhmacher, Stephan (Eds.) (1994). *The encyclopedia of Eastern philosophy and religion: Buddhism, Hinduism, Taoism, Zen.* Boston, MA: Shambhala.

3 Longgu

Conceptualizing the Human Person from the Inside Out

Deborah Hill

1 Introduction

Across languages, the human person is conceptualized as being composed of a body that is visible and something else that is not (Wierzbicka, 1989, 2016). Longgu[1] is no exception: in this Oceanic language spoken on Guadalcanal, Solomon Islands, the human person is thought of as consisting of two parts, one of which is referred to as *suli* ('body') and the other one as *anoa* (roughly, 'spirit'). After a brief section on Longgu language and culture, followed by a review and dismissal of other contenders for the role played by the concept of *anoa*, this chapter discusses the Longgu conceptualization of the human person. Using Minimal English (Goddard, 2018a, 2018b: Chapter 9; see also the editor's postscript), it then explicates the concept of *anoa* and other culture-specific terms relevant to the discussion of the human person. It concludes that the conceptualization of the human person in Longgu can be described as seeing a human person 'from the inside out': rather than conceptualizing the human person as something visible (a body), with something invisible inside the body, Longgu people think of a human person in terms of what is inside (a 'spirit'), and then as what can be seen on the outside (a body).

In Longgu culture, spirits in general play a very important role. There are in fact two Longgu words for 'spirit', reflecting two kinds of 'spirit': one that is part of a human person and is inside the person (*anoa*), and another one that is associated with clans and families (*agalo*). The term for the second kind of spirit (*agalo*) can be loosely glossed in English as 'ancestor spirit'. It is ancestor spirits, and related concepts, that have received attention in the limited literature on Longgu (see Section 2) and in studies of the beliefs and ethnopsychologies of other Pacific cultures (e.g. Codrington, 1891; Hogbin, 1939[1969]; Keesing, 1982; White & Kirkpatrick, 1985). While this chapter focusses on the concept of *anoa* 'spirit' in Longgu, I will show that it is impossible to understand the concept of *anoa* 'spirit' without also trying to comprehend the concept of *agalo* 'ancestor spirit'.

It is hoped that the Longgu evidence presented in this chapter will contribute to the wider discussion on personhood in Melanesian anthropology. One of the most significant concepts in Melanesian anthropology is that of the Melanesian person as 'dividual' as opposed to the European person, who is 'individual' (Strathern, 1988; Mosko, 2010; Smith, 2012; Robbins, 2015). The first to introduce the idea of a concept of Melanesian personhood that is something other than 'individual' was Marilyn Strathern (1988: 13), who famously declared that 'Far from being regarded as unique entities, Melanesian persons are as dividually as they are individually conceived. They contain a generalized sociality within'. The extensive literature on this topic describes and discusses what has come to be known as *dividualism* from several perspectives. One relates primarily to kinship, another one to the cycle of life and death (Smith, 2012). The dividual person is relational, insofar as a person's conception of themselves is very much determined in relation to others, living and dead. The dividual person is 'permeable', while the individual is 'impermeable'. That is, the Melanesian concept of the human person is argued to be one that is less bound by the human body. The significance of spirits in the Longgu conceptualization of the human person points in the same direction.

2 Longgu Language and Culture

The Longgu community is divided into five matrilineal clans who share the same language. A member of the Southeast Solomonic subgroup of Oceanic languages (Lynch et al., 2002), it is a small language (around 3,000 speakers), with little in the way of documentation and materials. The primary source of information on the topic at hand comes from my own fieldwork and from discussions I have had over several decades with language consultants, especially Ben Livu, Gabriel Ropovono, and Matilda Matala. In addition to my own grammar of the language (Hill, 2011), there is one fairly extensive ethnographic study of the Longgu people, written by the anthropologist Ian Hogbin and published in 1964. The 1964 publication is based on fieldwork Hogbin carried out in 1933, when he lived in Longgu district for a period of three months (see also Hogbin, 1936). Because sources are so limited, the discussion in this chapter also draws on ethnographic material written about two closely related languages, Kwaio (Keesing, 1982) and Toqabaqita (Hogbin, 1939[1969]), both spoken on the nearby island of Malaita, and on comparative lexical data from related Oceanic languages and from Proto-Oceanic (Ross et al., 2016).

Longgu people today are overwhelmingly Christian. Different Christian denominations are associated with each of the main villages in the district. The majority of people are Anglican, but in addition there is a significant Seventh Day Adventist village, and there are smaller Catholic and South Sea Evangelical communities. In contrast, more than 80 years ago, Ian Hogbin reported that about half of the community were professing Christians and that, at the same time, traditional practices such as magic were regularly performed by older men as 'the higher missionary officers have been content to leave the conversion of the district in the hands of native teachers', and 'the new doctrines have not penetrated very deeply' (Hogbin, 1936: 243). Nonetheless, evidence from Hogbin (1939[1969]) strongly suggests that the belief systems of Longgu people have interacted with Christianity and that there has been some integration of ways of thinking rather than an overtaking of one set of ideas by another. After leaving Longgu district in 1933, Hogbin's next field site was Toqabaqita in North Malaita. At several points in his ethnography of Toqabaqita, he makes comparisons with Longgu, arguing that each society's view of Christianity owes as much 'to the natives themselves as to missionaries' (1939[1969]: 227). For example, when referring to the Malaitan belief that God, like *akalo* (cognate with Longgu *agalo*), is responsible for diseases, he points out that Longgu people do not believe that God punishes sin with death as they do not believe that *agalo* cause death (1939[1969]: 228).

Contact with Christianity over many years has undeniably created a more complex situation in terms of the Longgu conceptualization of personhood, just as it has for other Melanesian societies (Mosko, 2015; Nanau, 2017): the term *anoa* 'spirit', discussed here, is also the term used for 'soul' in the Christian Church. In this chapter, to distinguish traditional beliefs from Christian beliefs, I maintain 'spirit' as a gloss for *anoa*, rather than 'soul'. In the context of the Longgu conceptualization of the human person, the concept of *anoa* is not identical to the concept of the Christian soul. It does not have a moral component. In addition, because of the important relationship between the two types of spirit in Longgu, *anoa* 'spirit' and *agalo* 'ancestor spirit' (discussed later), a relationship that is not part of the Christian understanding of 'soul', the term 'spirit' is more appropriate.

From a linguistic point of view, the most important observation for the purposes of this chapter is that Longgu has two types of possessive constructions (Hill, 2011). These are the direct possessive construction, in which a possessive suffix is directly attached to the possessor noun, and a possessive construction in which a possessive pronoun follows the possessor noun. The two construction types are also known as the inalienable and alienable possessive constructions, although these semantic labels do not always reflect the exact semantic relationship. Kinship terms, for example, do not fit the pattern of an association between directly possessed nouns and close family relationships. Thus, the words for 'mother', 'father', and 'mother's brother/sister's child', all of which express close relationships, are used in alienable possessive constructions (e.g. *tia nau* 'my mother', *mama nau* 'my father', *sa'i nau* 'my mother's brother/my sister's child'). Nevertheless, direct (inalienable) possession *is* typically used when there is a close relationship between the possessor and possessee: body part terms, such as *bou* 'head', and abstract concepts closely linked to humans, such as *hanahana* 'thinking', for instance, enter into direct possessive constructions (e.g. *bou-na* 'his/her head', *hanahana-na* 'his/her thinking'). Similarly, the Longgu words for 'body', *suli*, and 'spirit', *anoa*, are directly possessed nouns, e.g. *suli-na* 'his/her body', *anoa-na* 'his/her spirit'. In addition, other Longgu terms that will be discussed as possible contenders for the part of a person inside the body, e.g. *nunu* 'shadow', enter into direct possessive constructions.

Inalienable possession, as a semantic notion rather than a grammatical category, is also important in the discussion of the boundaries of personhood in Melanesia, especially with regard to exchange relationships (Weiner, 1992). Analysing the relationship between the possessor and the inalienably possessed physical object that forms part of an exchange includes the question of whether objects that are deemed to be inalienably possessed reflect possession in relation to the person or possession of the object as a reflection of personal relations. The latter view is in keeping with the view that Melanesian persons are dividual in the sense of relational (see earlier).

3 Why *Anoa* 'Spirit'?

The ethnographic and comparative linguistic material referred to earlier suggests that there may be Longgu terms other than *anoa* 'spirit' that should be considered as possible candidates for denoting the part of the human person inside the person. In this section, I introduce these terms and explain why they should be considered. I then go on to argue that there is strong evidence that the term for the part inside of the human person in Longgu is indeed *anoa*. Ethnographic research by Hogbin appears to indicate that the part of a human person inside a person in Longgu is *nunu* 'shadow':

> The natives refer to a person's shadow and his reflection in a mirror or a forest pool by the same term, *nunu*. At death, but not before, so they say, both become spirits, respectively the *anggalo* and the *anoa*. The former possesses *nanama* ['power'; see Section 5] and remains around the village, whereas the latter, like the Christian soul, passes to another world (located on the rocky island of Marapa off the eastern end of Guadalcanal) and takes no further interest in human concerns. *Anggalo* of the dead, normally invisible, may show themselves as fireflies, which are greatly feared.
>
> (Hogbin, 1964: 83; information in square brackets added by D.H.)

Hogbin's description suggests that *nunu* 'shadow' includes a meaning component similar to spirit, and that *anoa* is a spirit that comes once a person dies. Supporting evidence for this suggestion comes from Sa'a, another Southeast Solomonic language. The word *nunu* in Sa'a is glossed as 'shadow of persons, reflection, likeness, soul, consciousness' (Ross et al., 2016: 204). Further afield, some languages of Papua New Guinea (e.g. Manambu; see Aikhenvald, 2015) have terms for 'spirit' that also have the meaning of 'shadow'. It could therefore very well be the case that, in the 1930s, when Hogbin was living in Longgu, the term *nunu* 'shadow' included a spiritual aspect. However, consultants today say that it does not. Keeping in mind Roger Keesing's observation, in his 1982 study of the language and culture of the Kwaio people (who, like the Toqabaqita, live in North Malaita), that 'ideas about the soul and about the Land of the Dead [...] seem to be of marginal interest, and hence inconsistent, contradictory, and variable among individuals' (Keesing, 1982: 105), it seems plausible that information from consultants gathered 80 years apart is at least potentially inconsistent. On the other hand, as Hogbin did not speak the language and was there for a relatively short time (three months), it may be that his account did not, and does not, accurately reflect the Longgu conceptualization of a human person. In either case, Longgu consultants do not now understand the human person as being made up of a body (*suli*) and a shadow (*nunu*), and the two spirits referred to in Hogbin's extract are not seen as arising from a person's *nunu* 'shadow'. The other word that may be considered as a possible contender for the inside part of the human person is *hanahana* 'think-think'. This reduplicated form of the verb *hana* 'think' also functions as a verb, meaning 'thinking'. In addition, it can act as a noun and, as such, become the possessee of a direct possessive construction (*hanahana-mu* 'your thinking'). In its nominal form, it is commonly used and is translated in Solomons Pijin, the language of wider communication in the Solomon Islands, as *tingting,* which has as one of its meanings 'mind'. When Longgu people are asked to translate the English word *mind,* they provide *hanahana* as the appropriate Longgu equivalent. Nevertheless, *hanahana* 'think-think' is not seen as one of the two parts that make up a human person. To some extent, it may well be that *hanahana*'s ability to function grammatically as a noun as well as a verb, i.e. its linguistic features, leads to the perception that there is a 'mind' concept in Longgu. However, it is the translation of *hanahana* into English, rather than the meaning of the Longgu word, that suggests this. As it turns out, there is a high degree of ambiguity (action versus thing) in some uses of *hanahana.* It is a noun in *a'eni hanahanagi* 'important *hanahana*', a phrase that clearly does not lend itself to translation by means of the word *mind*; instead, *ideas* (as in *important ideas*) seems to provide a better fit. In *su'u hanahana* 'change (your) *hanahana*', it is in fact a verb; it could be translated as 'mind', but this is misleading and 'thinking' is more accurate. The possessive suffix *-da* in *va'a-meta hanahana-da* 'ease their *hanahana*' indicates that, here, we are dealing with a noun, which may favour translation by means of the English word *mind*; once again, though, 'thinking' seems to be a more appropriate gloss.

Thus, while Longgu has a word that can be translated by means of the English word *mind,* 'mind' is not its primary meaning, and this word does not reflect one of the two parts of a human person. On the other hand, I can think of four reasons that suggest that *anoa* 'spirit' is the best candidate for the term referring to the part of the human person inside a person.

First of all, there is a word in Longgu (and there are cognates in some related languages) that can be glossed as 'body and spirit'. Like the other words that have been discussed so far, it forms part of a directly possessed nominal construction. The word is *zabe* and language consultants describe the concept behind it as made up of two things: *anoa* 'spirit' and *suli* 'body'. It is not made up of *nunu* 'shadow' and *suli* 'body', nor *hanahana* 'think-think' and *suli* 'body'. The word *zabe* thus provides good evidence of what the non-visible part of the human person is in Longgu: it has to be *anoa*.

Second, there is a close conceptual relationship between *anoa* 'spirit' and *agalo* 'ancestor spirit', but it is not the one noted by Ian Hogbin in the previous excerpt. He reported that there are two types of spirits in Longgu (as there are in some other Austronesian languages, e.g. North Mekeo, in Papua New Guinea; cf. Mosko, 2010: 229), and that both come from *nunu* 'shadow' at the time of death. While my own research does not support the latter claim, it reveals a conceptual relationship of a different chronological nature: *anoa* 'spirit' and *agalo* 'ancestor spirit' do not surface at the same time, but one becomes the other: *anoa* is the spirit of the person that *leaves* the person at the time of death and *becomes* a spirit of a different kind (*agalo*). This is discussed in detail later.

Third, *anoa* includes a meaning component that, in Minimal English, can be expressed as 'because of this something inside this someone [i.e., because of their *anoa*], this someone can live'; this suggests that *anoa* is part of a human person (but different from the body, which is the visible, exterior, part).

Finally, according to Longgu speaker Gabriel Ropovono (pers. comm.), there is no Solomons Pijin translation for *anoa* 'spirit' or *zabe* 'body and spirit', reinforcing the point that these are deeply cultural terms that are meaningful within Longgu culture but are not more widely shared. Longgu *anoa* is culture-specific; Longgu people have a shared understanding of what it means to talk about their and each other's *anoa*. In contrast, *hanahana* 'think-think' has the Solomons Pijin for *tingting* (from English *think-think*) and *nunu* has the Pijin form *sado* (from English 'shadow').

Having argued that the human person in Longgu is conceptualized as being made up of a body (*suli*) and spirit (*anoa*), the next section discusses and explicates the meaning of the word *anoa*, not in isolation, but with reference to the person whose *anoa* it is. In other words, what will be explicated is not the word *anoa* as such, but the phrase 'someone's *anoa*'.

4 *Anoa* 'Spirit'

Together, *anoa* 'spirit' and *suli* 'body' make up a human person. Every Longgu person is born with both a *suli* 'body' and an *anoa* 'spirit'. Someone's *anoa* is something everyone knows a person has inside of them, and that no one can see or touch. When one speaks of someone's *anoa* 'spirit', it is conceived of as being inside their *zabe* 'body and spirit'. This is expressed in Example 1:

1 *Tuhuna*   *inoni-gi*   *ara*   **anoa**-*na*   *ubu-na*

  every   person-PL   3PL.SBJ spirit-3SG.POSS inside-3SG.POSS

  zabe-na

  body.spirit-3SG.POSS

  'Every person has a spirit inside his/her 'body and spirit''.

Every time a new person is born, there is a new spirit (*anoa*). When a person dies, his or her *anoa* 'spirit' leaves the person and goes to a place, Marapa, a small island not too far from the Longgu area. This place was also referred to in Hogbin's report, earlier. At Marapa, this spirit becomes a spirit of a different kind: an *agalo* 'ancestor spirit'. While *anoa* 'spirit' is connected to an individual, evident linguistically through its behaviour as part of a direct possessive construction (e.g. *anoa-na* 'his/her spirit'; *anoa-mu* 'your spirit'), *agalo* 'spirit' relates to the spirits of a clan line or family. *Anoa* 'spirit' is not a term used frequently in everyday language but it is *anoa*, like *birrimbirr* in Yolngu and *sind* 'mind' in Danish (see the discussion in Wierzbicka, 2016: 452–453), that is the term particular to Longgu culture.

Anoa shares meaning elements of Danish *sjoel*. Levisen (2017: 133) argues that Danish *sjoel* 'soul' 'does not seem to be a moral concept' and that 'a *sjoel* is what makes a person unique' (Levisen, 2017: 133). Similarly, someone's *anoa* does not have a moral component in the way a person's soul does in English, and it is someone's *anoa* that makes a Longgu person unique. Ben Livu, Longgu Paramount Chief, described the relationship between *suli* 'body' and *anoa* 'spirit' as one of working together. Someone's *suli* 'body' cannot work without the *anoa* 'spirit'. Someone's *anoa* 'spirit' cannot work without the *suli* 'body'. When the body dies, the spirit leaves.

Longgu *anoa* 'spirit' shares some meaning components with Yolngu *birrimbirr*, too. For example, Wierzbicka's (2016: 472) explication of Yolngu *birrimbirr* includes the components 'this something is something very good', and 'because there is this something inside this someone, this someone can live', which is also part of the Longgu concept *anoa* 'spirit'. This component is captured in the explication for *anoa* 'spirit', to be provided later. However, the components 'people can know that it is like this: some time before this someone was born, this part of this someone was part of a place where some people lived before', and 'after this someone dies, this part of this someone can be part of the same place', which are part of the meaning of Yolngu *birrimbirr*, have no equivalent in the Longgu concept of *anoa* 'spirit'. The Longgu *anoa* does not come from someone else; in addition, within the Longgu community there is a shared understanding of where someone's *anoa* goes when a person dies, and it is not a place where 'some people lived before'.

While there is a change from *anoa* 'someone's spirit' to *agalo* 'ancestor spirit' after a person's death, people can still refer to someone's *anoa* 'spirit' after this someone has died, as shown in Example 2. People can speak of their dead relative's *anoa* as having power or influence over them, particularly at a time of sickness. This relationship between sickness, healing, and the influence of spirits in a person's life has been noted in other cultures and is an example of a dividualist understanding of life (Robbins, 2015: 181).

2   **Anoa-da**   *ara*   *aro-vi-a*   *ngaia*   *e*

    spirit-3PL.POSS   3PL.SBJ   sorry-TRS-3SG.OBJ   3SG   3SG.SBJ

    mata'i   *ania.*

    sick   INSTR-3SG.OBJ

    'Their spirits feel sorry for him, he's sick because of it'.

To reflect the earlier discussion of *anoa* 'spirit', I propose the explication that follows. The template I use is a slight variation on the one proposed by Wierzbicka (2016). It starts off with the phrase that is being explicated, i.e. *someone's X*, and comprises four blocks ([A], [B], [C], and [D]), respectively titled *What it is, How this someone can think about this something, What this something is like* (rather than *What this part of someone is like*), and *What people can know about this something* (rather than *What people can know about this part of someone*). It contains information that is not specifically referred to in the previous discussion but that should nonetheless be self-explanatory and that is, in some instances, part of any ethnopsychological personhood construct (EPC) in any language denoting a part of someone that is not part of that someone's body but is inside that someone. In block [A], someone's *anoa* is described as '*something* inside this someone' and in the line that follows as 'this *something* is part of this someone'. This is in line with the formulations adopted by Wierzbicka, but it is nonetheless important to stress that, while it is part of someone, someone's *anoa* is clearly seen as 'something'. Therefore, where possible, I have preferred the wording 'something' rather than 'part of someone' (or 'part of me') in subsequent lines of the explication.

someone's *anoa* 'spirit'

[A] [WHAT IT IS]

something inside this someone

this something is part of this someone

this something is not part of this someone's body

people cannot see this something

people cannot touch this something

this something is something very good

because of this something inside this someone, this someone can live

[B] [HOW THIS SOMEONE CAN THINK ABOUT THIS SOMETHING]

this someone can think about this something like this:

    'this something is part of me

    because of this something, I can do many things, I can think many things, I can feel many things'

[C] [WHAT THIS SOMETHING IS LIKE]

this something is not like anything else

because it is inside people, people are not like other creatures

something like this is not inside other creatures

[D] [WHAT PEOPLE CAN KNOW ABOUT THIS SOMETHING]

people can know that it is like this:

> when someone is born, this something is inside this someone; this something was not inside someone else before this someone was born
>
> when someone dies, this something does not die
>
> at the same time, this something is not inside this someone anymore, it is in another place
>
> this other place is called Marapa
>
> when this something is not inside this someone anymore, this something becomes something of another kind
>
> this something of another kind is called agalo

5 *Agalo* 'Ancestor Spirit'

The word *agalo* refers to spirits in general, and to ancestor spirits in particular. Among Christians, the word *agalo* is also used for the Holy Spirit, i.e. *Agalo Abu* (lit. 'spirit sacred').

Most spirits were originally someone's ancestor spirit. However, Codrington (1891: 124) notes that, in the Solomon Islands, it is difficult to get a definition of a spirit, but there are some spirits that were never human ('never men, and have not the bodily nature of a man').[2] One example Codrington gives is of the spirit Koevasi, who is still known by Longgu people today. Koevasi is 'asserted there to be superhuman, never alive with a mere human life, and therefore not now a ghost; one that now receives no worship, but is the subject of stories only, without any religious consideration' (*ibid.*). Koevasi is female: 'How she came into existence no one knows; she made things of all kinds; she became herself the mother of a woman from whom the people of the island descend' (*ibid.*).

In the context of this discussion, I will not propose an explication for the kind of spirit that has never been human, but I will provide one for *agalo* 'ancestor spirit'. The word does not form part of a possessive construction, which means that *agalo* is not part of someone. The word *agalo* 'spirit' can be modified, reflecting the belief that there are many kinds of spirits, e.g. *agalo wasi* 'wild spirit', *agalo asi* 'sea spirit', and so on. Spirits can be female, as attested by the phrase *agalo geni* 'spirit woman'.

Agalogi 'spirits' are associated with clans and locations and can take different forms, including the form of an animal, such as a *beasavu* 'shark', or something not human, such as an *omeo* 'water baby'. *Agalogi* 'spirits' occur frequently in texts about how a clan began. In Example 3, the 'spirit' could not be considered an ancestor spirit as it was a spirit that came before people.

3   *Vuni-vuni-a-na-ina*   *te*   **agalo**   *mola*   *nina*   *ta-na*
   begin-RED-NOM-DEIC   one   spirit   only   DEIC   LOC-3SG.POSS

   mole   *sina-gi-na.*
   all   line-PL-DEIC

   'At the beginning, there was only one spirit then for all of those lines/clans'.

Some texts show people being tricked by *agalogi* 'spirits'. In Example 4, a water baby (*omeo*) pretending to be a girl brought to the village for marriage finds her way back to the village to show the groom that *she* is his bride. The different forms that spirits take are associated with different clans. For instance, stories that include *omeo* 'water baby' are common to the Zibo clan of Longgu. In this story, the *omeo* 'water baby' comes from Marapa, the land of the dead, indicating that it is an ancestor spirit.

4   *m-e*   *bere-zai-a*   *burunga-na*   *mi*   *ngaia*
   CONJ-3SG.SBJ   see-know-3SG.OBJ   spouse-3SG.POSS   CONJ   3SG.PRO

   na   *a'aeni*   *geni*   *ara*   *voli-a*   *wini-u*
   FOC   real   woman   3PL.SBJ   buy-3SG.OBJ   DAT-1SG.OBJ

   nenena.
   DEIC

   agalo-i   *ra'o*   *nu*   *la bwani-a*   *mai*   *komu-i-na*
   spirit-SG   maybe   1SG.SBJ   go from-3SG.OBJ   hither   village-SG-DEIC

   'And he recognized his wife. She was the real woman they bought for him there. Perhaps it was the spirit that I bought back from that village'.

As noted earlier, *agalogi* 'spirits' are associated with different loca-tions. While the island of Marapa is the place where ancestor spirits stay, other locations are also associated with particular spirits, as in Example 5). When a person dies, the spirit goes to Marapa, but from there some spirits move to other locations.[3] In most cases, this is for a short time; however, to give but one example, if a significant person in a clan's history was known to live at a certain place, then the spirit sometimes returns and stays there.

5   *m-e*   *zudu*   *i*   *Bo'o*   *ta-na*   *vu'a*   *ni*

    CONJ-3SG.SBJ   sit   LOC   place   LOC-3SG.POSS   place   ASS

    agalo-i-*na*

    spirit-SG-DEIC

    'And she sits at Bo'o at the place of that spirit'.

Hogbin describes *agalo* as follows:

> [T]he natives believe in the existence of three different kinds of supernatural beings, the spirits of the dead, spirits which can at will become incarnate as sharks, and snake spirits. The spirits of the dead and the shark spirits are both called *ang-galo*, while the snake spirits are known as *vi'ona*. The natives hold that these are all possessed by power which they can use for the benefit of human beings. This power is given a special name, *nanama*. It is an attribute of all spirits, like their ability to remain invisible and to move about from place to place with extreme speed, and has no ultimate source. With regard to an-cestral spirits, the more important a man was in life the greater his *nanama* is supposed to be after his death.
>
> (Hogbin, 1936: 244)

Nanama refers to the concept of *mana* 'spiritual power' known through-out the Pacific. The meaning and use of the term *mana* in different Melanesian and Polynesian societies has developed over time (Hogbin, 1936; Keesing, 1982; Blust, 2007; Tomlinson & Tengan, 2016). Hogbin makes it clear that *nanama* is not something that is part of a person, but part of a spirit. Keesing (1982) describes *mana* as a word that is used primarily as a verb; it is therefore not a 'thing'. He places it within a paradigm that also includes Kwaio verbs, such as *abu* '(be) taboo' and *mola* '(be) ordinary'. My own understanding of how the cognate terms are used in Longgu reflects Keesing's description of things or people "being taboo and being ordinary". Something or someone is *mana* or *abu* in relation to someone or something else. For the purposes of this discussion, it is important to note the relationship between *agalo* 'spirit' and *mana*, and their interactions with someone's life. Hogbin (1936) also notes that all spirits are invisible, but that they can change forms at times. This ability to change forms has been seen in Example 4 and is also illustrated in Example 6, from the same story. In this example, the girl is knocked down by an *omeo* 'water baby' and prevented from getting back into the canoe with the boys. Instead, the *omeo* takes on the form of the girl, and the boys take her back to the village. After some time, they realize that she is not the 'real woman' but one type of spirit woman instead.

6	*aralu*	*leta*	*ania*		*geni-na*	
	3PAU.SBJ	doubt	INSTR-3SG.OBJ		woman-DEIC	

geni	*golu*	*la*	*volia*	*mai*	*Marapa-i-na*
woman	3PAU	go	buy-3SG.OBJ	hither	Marapa-SG.DEIC

se	*bere*	*ade.una.ta'e*
NEG	look	in.that.way

se	*ade.una.ta'e*	*bo-bosa-a-na*
NEG	in.that.way	RED-speak-NOM-3SG.POSS

m-e	*se*	*bere*	*ade.una.tae*	*suli-na*
CONJ-3SG.SBJ	NEG	look	in.that.way	body-3SG.POSS

'They doubted about that woman, the woman we bought from Marapa. She did not look like that, she did not speak like that, and her body did not look like that'.

Although not strictly speaking a personhood construct since *agalo* is never part of a person, it may be advantageous to use a template for the explication that is as close as possible to the one used before, for *anoa*. This is what I have done in the following. Changes are minimal: there is no verb *can* in the captions of blocks [B] and [D]. The explication takes into account the *agalogi*'s ability to assume a different form (animal or human) (cf., in block [C], the component 'this something can become something of another kind for a short time'). Hogbin's observation that the spirits can move around "at extreme speed" and that they are normally invisible is also supported by my own field work and is accounted for in blocks [A] and [C]. Information about the *agalogi*'s home (Marapa) is found in block [B]. The association between *agalo* and clan lines is also the object of block [B], which relies on the concepts of 'mother', 'mother's mother', and 'mother's mother's mother'. As a matrilineal society, Longgu people belong to the clan of their mother, and the spirits are associated with particular clans.

agalo **'ancestor spirit'**

[A] [WHAT IT IS]

something

people cannot see this something

people cannot touch this something

at some time before now, this something was someone's anoa

when this someone died, this someone's anoa became this something

[B] [HOW PEOPLE THINK ABOUT THIS SOMETHING]

people think about this something like this:

    this something is in a place called Marapa

    this something is in this place with many other things of the same kind

    people can know one thing of this kind, not many, because at one time it was someone's anoa

    if two people can say about the same woman: "This woman is my mother",

        these two know the same thing of this kind

    if two people can say about the same woman: "This woman is my mother's mother",

        these two know the same thing of this kind

    if two people can say about the same woman: "This woman is my mother's mother's mother",

        these two know the same thing of this kind

    if two people know the same thing of this kind, they know they are like one thing

[C] [WHAT THIS SOMETHING IS LIKE]

this something can move to another place for a short time

this something can move to this place in a very short time

this something can become something of another kind for a short time

[D] [WHAT PEOPLE KNOW ABOUT THIS SOMETHING]

people know that it is like this:

when this something becomes something of another kind, people can see this something

this something can do bad things to people

this something can be near people

it can be like this when someone is sick

it can be like this at other times

6 *Zabe* 'Body and Spirit'

In Sections 4 and 5, I have discussed the cultural context of the two types of spirits referred to by Ian Hogbin, viz. the *anoa* 'spirit', which is part of a human person, and the *agalo* 'ancestor spirit', which is what the *anoa* becomes after a person's death. I have proposed explications for both. In this section, I provide more information about a concept that was briefly mentioned in Section 3, where, based on glosses of cognate forms in other languages, it was glossed as 'body and spirit'. The concept in question is *zabe*.

Zabe refers to the body and spirit (*suli va'inia anoai*) taken together. *Zabe* is a noun that can enter into a possessive construction, i.e. it can occur with a third person singular possessive suffix such as *-na*, which results in the phrase *zabe-na* 'his/her body and spirit'. As my Longgu colleagues said, the body cannot work without the spirit, and the spirit cannot work without the body; when the body dies, the spirit goes. When asked about the components of *zabe*, Longgu consultants categorically rejected any suggestion that *zabe* could refer to body and mind (**suli va'inia hanahanai*) or body and shadow (**suli va'inia nunui*).

As *zabe* 'body and spirit' refers to both the inside and outside parts of the human person, we might ask why this is not the word for 'person'. The word for person in Longgu is *inoni*. Cognates of this form (e.g. *tinoni, sinoni, inoni*) are widely attested as the word for 'person' in Southeast as well as Northwest Solomonic languages. As Ross et al. (2016: 48) note, the term 'apparently has now become the general term for a human being'. In Longgu, *inoni* 'person' is a very frequently occurring word. Its plural form is *inonigi* 'people'. *Inoni* 'person' can be modified with an adjective to refer, for example, to a 'good person' (*inoni metai*) or a 'bad person' (*inoni ta'ai*). The semantic prime SOMEONE can be rendered in Longgu as *te inoni* 'one person, someone'. In contrast, *zabe* is a possessed noun, that is, it must be referred to as 'someone's *zabe*'. It is more semantically complex than *inoni* 'person' and cannot be used as a lexicalization for the semantic prime SOMEONE.

At the same time, glossing *zabe* as 'body and spirit' does not fully capture the meaning of the word since it is possible to say:

7   *Anoa-na*   *ubu-na*   ***zabe-na***

    spirit-3SG.POSS   inside-3SG.POSS   body.and.spirit-3SG.POSS

    'His spirit is inside his 'body and spirit''.

For purposes of comparison, we can look at the Proto East Oceanic (PEOc) form **[q]abe* 'body' and the Proto-South East Solomonic (SES) form **[q]abe* 'body, bulk' (Ross et al., 2016: 81). A number of SES languages have similar forms cognate with *zabe* referring to body, bulk, or trunk of a tree. The closely related language Sa'a, for instance, has *sabe* 'body, trunk, mass'. Further afield, **abe* refers to Proto-North Central Vanuatu (NCV) 'body incl. spiritual and other less tangible aspects' and one NCV language, Lakon, has the form *epe-* 'body and soul'. Like the Longgu and Sa'a terms, these nouns enter into possessive constructions. Similar to the NCV languages, but unlike other SES languages, the meaning of the Longgu word *zabe* includes a 'spiritual aspect'. From this discussion, we can say that in Longgu *zabe* is 'something' rather than 'someone', as it is possessed by 'someone'. This is reflected in the following explication proposed.

someone's *zabe* 'body and spirit'

[A] [WHAT IT IS]

something

this something has two parts

one part is someone's body, the other part is inside this someone

[B] [WHAT PEOPLE KNOW ABOUT THIS SOMETHING]

when this someone lives, it is like this:

the two parts of this something live

the body cannot live if the something inside this someone is not inside this someone

the something inside this someone cannot live if it is not inside this someone

after this someone dies, it is like this:

the two parts of this something are not in the same place anymore

when the body dies, the other part is in another place

this place is called Marapa

when the other part is in this place, it becomes something of another kind

this something of another kind is called agalo

7 More on Marapa

The island of Marapa, which as we saw is not far from Longgu in the Marau Sound, on the north-east tip of Guadalcanal, is very important culturally. More generally, place is very important in personhood constructs in Melanesia. People's identity is linked to their place or home (Strathern, 1988: 80; Lindstrom, 2013: 246). Nanau (2017: 184), in a discussion of the conception of personhood in Lengo, notes the importance of taking into account the physical environment to provide a complete picture of personhood. Smith (2012: 53), too, makes the point, in his explanation of the term *dividual*, that dividuals are seen to have a deep and intrinsic connection to a particular place. The concept of the 'place of the dead' is also seen in a number of discussions of Melanesian spirits (e.g. Codrington, 1891; Hogbin, 1939[1969]; Keesing, 1982; Hess, 2006). It is not surprising, then, that the Longgu conception of *agalo* 'spirit', too, includes something about the 'place' where the spirit goes after death and lives. Ethnographic studies of other Solomon Islands communities reveal that, in this geographical region, it is common for societies to have an island as the place of the dead, or the spirit island, and that there are shared locations for different language groups. In North Malaita, for example, Toqabaqita (Hogbin, 1939[1969]: 110) and Kwaio (Keesing, 1982: 110) refer to an island called Anonggwau (Hogbin) or Anogwa'u (Keesing), located between Malaita and Santa Ysabel islands, as their spirit island. Similarly, Marapa, or the general area of Marau that is made up of many small islands, is known as the spirit island not just by Longgu people but also by Lengo people of Guadalcanal (Paul Unger, pers. comm.), by people of Sa'a on the southern end of Malaita (Codrington, 1891), and by people of the island of Florida (Gela) (Codrington, 1891). According to Codrington (1891), Marapa consists of two islands and the spirits live a life that resembles the life of the living:[4]

> The ghostly inhabitants of Marapa live something like a worldly life; the children chatter and annoy the elder ghosts, so they are placed apart upon the second island; men and women ghosts are together, they have houses, gardens, and canoes, yet all is unsubstantial. Living men cross to Marapa and see nothing; but there is water there in which laughter and cries are heard; there are places where water is seen to have been disturbed, and the banks are wet as if bathers had been there.
>
> (Codrington, 1891: 260)

My own fieldwork has not revealed Marapa as being two islands, but it does reflect Codrington's account of a place where the spirits' lives recall those of the living. Marapa occurs in stories about clans, as in Example 6, and it appears in stories about how clans or subclans began. It has been included in the explications of the three words discussed so far: *anoa* 'spirit', *agalo* 'spirit', and *zabe* 'body and spirit'. Because of its cultural significance in understanding how Longgu people conceptualize the human person, it requires its own explication:

Marapa

[A] [WHAT IT IS]

a place

this place is an island

this place is not far from the place where people live

many people can see this place

this place is where someone's *anoa* 'spirit' goes when someone dies this place is where someone's *anoa* 'spirit' becomes someone's *agalo* 'ancestor spirit'

this place is where someone's *agalo* 'ancestor spirit' is after this someone dies

[B] [WHAT PEOPLE THINK ABOUT THIS PLACE]

many people think like this about this place:

'a short time after someone dies, this someone's *anoa* is in this place

at the time when someone's *anoa* is in this place, this someone's *anoa* becomes something of another kind

this something is called *agalo*

there are many things of this kind [*agalogi*] in this place'

some people think like this about this place:

'this place is like the places where we live

it has the same kinds of things we have

the *agalogi* in this place live like we live

agalogi can move to other places in a very short time

they can move to the places where we live

they cannot be in these places for a long time'

8 Conclusion

As Anna Wierzbicka (2016: 452) notes in her discussion of the concepts of Danish *sind*, English *mind*, and Yolngu *birrimbirr*, '[i]n each linguistic sphere, such shared verbal currency establishes a level of verbal communication which is language- and culture-specific, and which binds speakers of a particular community as members of a single verbal economy'. For Longgu, this 'shared verbal currency' resides in the word *anoa* 'spirit'. The Longgu people conceptualize the human person as being made up of two parts, but the focus is not on a body (something outside) and then a spirit (something inside); rather, it is important to see the spirit as something that works with the body and then leaves the human person, to become a spirit of a different kind, at the time of death.

Our analysis, based on ethnographic and linguistic evidence, will hopefully contribute to the wider discussion of personhood and personhood constructs in Melanesian societies. The Longgu conceptualize the human person in a movement that goes from the inside (*anoa* 'spirit') to the outside (*suli* 'body'). Understanding the concept of *anoa* 'spirit' in Longgu requires an understanding of other important cultural concepts, such as *zabe* 'body and spirit', *agalo* 'ancestor spirit', and *Marapa*, the place of ancestor spirits. I have attempted to explicate these terms in an effort to show how Longgu people conceptualize the human person.

Acknowledgements

This chapter has benefitted from comments on an earlier draft by Felix Ameka, and from detailed comments and editing by Bert Peeters. I am very grateful to the two anonymous reviewers who provided detailed and constructive suggestions that helped to further develop the chapter. In particular, I thank Gabriel Ropovono and Matilda Maitala and the late Ben Livu for sharing their language and culture with me. I also acknowledge the discussions I was fortunate enough to have, at different times and many years ago, about culture, spirits, and religion in Longgu, Kwaio, and Toqabaqita with Roger Keesing and especially Frank Lichtenberk.

Editor's Postscript: NSM versus Minimal English

Minimal English, rather than Natural Semantic Metalanguage (NSM), has been used in the explications in Deborah Hill's chapter. Minimal English is a recent offshoot of NSM. In one of his *Ten lectures on Natural Semantic Metalanguage*, Goddard (2018b: 268–269) explains the difference:

> Minimal English [...] is based on semantic primes and universal semantic molecules, because these words are known to be relatively simple and highly cross-translatable. But it is not a problem to add other words into Minimal English if they are important and there are good reasons to believe that they are largely cross-translatable, or else indispensable. Minimal English is a practical project. It is not dedicated to the idea of precise linguistic analysis.
>
> For example, consider a word like *government*. In many places in the world you need to use the word *government* to get across messages about community development, public health, and

international relations. Likewise, a word like *plastic* could be very important in discussing pollution. There are major problems in many parts of the world with plastic containers getting into the sea and causing environmental damage. The word *mosquitoes* might seem very inconsequential, but mosquitoes are bearers of some of the worst diseases in the world, so in the health context, Minimal English may need to use the word *mosquitoes*.

Words that are important in the Longgu context (e.g. *island* in the explication of the place name Marapa) had to be retained as the explications were devised to "make sense" to the Longgu community as well as to the greatest number of cultural outsiders. Islands play a paramount role in the lives and the cultural outlook of the inhabitants of the Solomons, a nation in the South Pacific that consists of hundreds of them. An explication that tries to do away with the word *island*, replacing it with references to a 'place of one kind' and to the idea that 'there is a lot of water on all sides of places of this kind' (cf. Bromhead, 2018: 104–106), will just not work.

Two other non-NSM words, *become* and *move* (as in *move to another place*), have been used in the explications in this chapter. The fact that someone's *anoa* changes into an *agalo* when this someone dies is culturally very important, and so is the idea that *agalo* are very dynamic and very fast. The argument is perhaps slightly less compelling than in the case of the word *island*, but trying to avoid verbs such as *become* and *move* would once again have compromised the inherent plausibility of the explications.

Notes

1 Three of the languages mentioned in this chapter have been given different names by some linguists and ethnographers. Longgu is called Kaoka by Hogbin (1964), Toqabaqita is identified as Malu'u by Hogbin (1939[1969]), and Lengo is referred to as Doku and Thathimboko by Nanau (2017).
2 I'm grateful to Paul Unger for bringing this to my attention.
3 Roger Keesing documented differing views from Kwaio people of what happens to the spirit of a Kwaio person when they die. One of the views he mentions is very similar to the Longgu description of a spirit that goes to the island of the dead but can then return to the village of the living: 'When we die our shades go to Anogwa'u; but even so they stay

80 *Deborah Hill*

here with us. [...] Even though Anogwa'u is across the sea, the shade goes there [...]. It goes there to Anogwa'u, comes back and stays in Kwaio' (1982: 106).

4 Hogbin (1939[1969]: 110) describes the spirit island of Anoggwau (Toqabaqita) in similar terms, as 'a pale replica of that of mortals'.

References

Aikhenvald, Alexandra Y. (2015). Body, mind, and spirit: What makes up a person in Manambu. *Studies in Language, 39*(1), 85–117. doi:10.1075/sl.39.1.04aik

Blust, Robert A. (2007). Proto-Oceanic *mana revisited. *Oceanic Linguistics, 46*(2), 404–423. doi:10.1353/ol.2008.0005

Bromhead, Helen (2018). *Landscape and culture – Cross-linguistic perspectives.* Amsterdam: John Benjamins. doi:10.1075/clscc.9

Codrington, Robert Henry (1891). *The Melanesians: Studies in their anthropology and folklore.* London: Clarendon Press.

Goddard, Cliff (Ed.) (2018a). *Minimal English for a global world: Improved communication using fewer words.* Cham: Palgrave Macmillan. doi:10.1007/978-3-319-62512-6

Goddard, Cliff (2018b). *Ten lectures on Natural Semantic Metalanguage: Exploring language, thought and culture using simple, translatable words.* Leiden: Brill. doi:10.1163/9789004357723

Hess, Sabine (2006). Strathern's Melanesian 'dividual' and the Christian 'individual': A perspective from Vanua Lava, Vanuatu. *Oceania, 76*(3), 285–296. doi:10.1002/j.1834-4461.2006.tb03058.x

Hill, Deborah (2011). *Longgu grammar.* Munich: Lincom.

Hogbin, H. Ian (1936). Mana. *Oceania, 6*(3), 241–274. doi:10.1002/j.1834-4461.1936.tb00187.x

Hogbin, H. Ian (1939[1969]). *Experiments in civilization: The effects of European culture on a native community of the Solomon Islands.* London: Routledge & Kegan Paul.

Hogbin, Ian (1964). *A Guadalcanal society: The Kaoka speakers.* Stanford, CA: Holt, Rinehart and Winston.

Keesing, Roger M. (1982). *Kwaio religion: The living and the dead in a Solomon Island society.* New York: Columbia University Press.

Levisen, Carsten (2017). Personhood constructs in language and thought: New evidence from Danish. In Zhengdao Ye (Ed.), *The semantics of nouns* (pp. 120–145). Oxford: Oxford University Press. doi:10.1093/oso/9780198736721.003.0005

Lindstrom, Lamont (2013). Agnes C.P. Watt and Melanesian personhood. *The Journal of Pacific History, 48*(3), 243–266. doi:10.1080/00223344.2013.832020

Lynch, John, Ross, Malcolm, & Crowley, Terry (2002). *The Oceanic languages.* Richmond, VA and Surrey: Curzon Press.

Mosko, Mark (2010). Partible penitents: Dividual personhood and Christian practice in Melanesia and the West. *Journal of the Royal Anthropological Institute, 16*(2), 215–240. doi:10.1111/j.1467-9655.2010.01618.x

Mosko, Mark (2015). Unbecoming individuals: The partible character of the Christian person. *HAU: Journal of Ethnographic Theory, 5*(1), 361–393. doi:10.14318/hau5.1.017

Nanau, Gordon Leua (2017). 'Na Vanuagu': Epistemology and person-hood in Tathimboko, Guadalcanal. In Upolu Lumā Vaai & Unaisi Nabobo-Baba (Eds.), *The relational self: Decolonising personhood in the Pacific* (pp. 177–201). Suva: University of the South Pacific Press & Pacific Theological College.

Robbins, Joel (2015). Dumont's hierarchical dynamism: Christianity and individualism revisited. *HAU: Journal of Ethnographic Theory, 5*(1), 173–195. doi:10.14318/hau5.1.009

Ross, Malcolm, Pawley, Andrew, & Osmond, Meredith (2016). *The lexicon of Proto Oceanic. The culture and environment of ancestral Oceanic society: Vol. 5. People: Body and mind.* Canberra: Asia-Pacific Linguistics.

Smith, Karl (2012). From dividual and individual selves to porous subjects. *The Australian Journal of Anthropology, 23*(1), 50–64. doi:10.11 11/j.1757-6547.2012.00167.x

Strathern, Marilyn (1988). *The gender of the gift: Problems with women and problems with society in Melanesia.* Berkeley, CA: University of California Press.

Tomlinson, Matt, & Tengan, Ty P. Kāwika (Eds.) (2016). *New mana: Transformations of a classic concept in Pacific languages and cultures.* Canberra: ANU Press. doi:10.22459/NM.04.2016

Weiner, Annette B. (1992). *Inalienable possessions: The paradox of keeping-while-giving.* Berkeley, CA: University of California Press.

White, Geoffrey M., & Kirkpatrick, John (Eds.) (1985). *Person, self, and experience: Exploring Pacific ethnopsychologies.* Berkeley, CA: University of California Press.

Wierzbicka, Anna (1989). Soul and mind: Linguistic evidence for ethnopsychology and cultural history. *American Anthropologist, 91*(1), 41–58. doi:10.1525/aa.1989.91.1.02a00030 – Revised and expanded in Anna Wierzbicka, *Semantics, culture, and cognition: Universal human concepts in culture-specific configurations* (pp. 31–63), New York, NJ: Oxford University Press, 1992.

Wierzbicka, Anna (2016). Two levels of verbal communication, universal and culture-specific. In Andrea Rocci & Louis de Saussure (Eds.), *Verbal communication* (pp. 447–482). Berlin: de Gruyter Mouton. doi:10.1515/9783110255478-024

4 Tracing the Thai 'Heart'

The Semantics of a Thai Ethnopsychological Construct

Chavalin Svetanant

1 Introduction

This chapter seeks to shed new light on just one of the many ethnopsychological personhood constructs (EPCs) encapsulated in the Thai language. As in the other chapters in this book, the term *ethnopsychological personhood construct* refers to items in the lexicon of a language for concepts such as 'the (nonphysical) heart', 'the mind', 'the soul', or 'the spirit'. Such constructs, cognitively real but physically invisible, are essential parts of a person: they complement, so to speak, the body, which does lend itself to physical observation. Often taken for granted, EPCs are anything but universal; the reality is that, analogous to other cultural key terms, they are culture-specific. They are folk concepts that are formulated differently across cultures and that are often untranslatable across languages.

One such untranslatable concept is the common monosyllabic Thai word *chai* ใจ, often glossed as 'heart'.[1] Moore (1992: 11) points out that if one wishes to understand how Thai people perceive themselves and the world around them, as well as their identity and cultural heritage, this is a concept that is nonetheless essential to understand:

> Whether you are a doctor, dock worker, lawyer, factory worker, merchant or jack-of-all-trades, then, you are pulling an oar in the same conceptual boat constructed from the same metaphors as everyone else in your language and culture. If you wish to row in the Thai conceptual boat, an understanding of **jai** is indispensable.

Chai is the only *indigenous* Thai term referring to an EPC; together with its frequency, this is the reason why it was selected for scrutiny

in this chapter.[2] Based on the Thai National Corpus (TNC) database, which, as of May 2013, comprised a total of 32,667,991 words
of written text, it ranks as the 166th most frequently used word in
the language; it occurred 28,101 times in various text types including fiction, non-fiction, and academic as well as non-academic texts,
making up 0.086% of the total number of TNC tokens. It shows up
4,138 times in *Si Phaen Din* 'Four Reigns' (1953), the longest and
best-known novel of Kukrit Pramoj, former Prime Minister and
distinguished author of many contemporary Thai works of literature. The total word count for this novel is 388,346, which means
chai appears once every 93 words.

The remainder of this chapter is structured as follows. Section 2
illustrates the multiple ways in which *chai* is used in contemporary Thai. An authoritative dictionary will be called upon to list
its meanings, as seen through lexicographers' eyes. The list will be
further illustrated with reference to conventional phrases and idioms, then expanded to account for unconventional usage (neolo-
gisms, slang) in song lyrics, online discussion forums, etc. Section 3
provides insight into the semantic development of the word from its
earliest attested uses in the 13th century to the present day, relying
on data from a wide range of classical and contemporary sources;
the aim is to establish the origins of at least some of the current uses
of the word *chai*. On the basis of the findings made in Sections 2
and 3, Section 4 then seeks to explicate the modern folk concept
of *chai*, a key cultural concept in Thai culture, using English and
Thai versions of the Natural Semantic Metalanguage (NSM). The
explication will be much more detailed than any existing semantic
descriptions of the term and will provide a starting point for future
comparative research into other EPCs present in Thai and/or in the
languages that Thai has been in contact with over the centuries.
Section 5 concludes the chapter.

2 *Chai* ใจ 'Heart' in Modern Thai

The National Dictionary of the Thai Royal Institute B.E. 2554
(2011) defines *chai* as 'an entity with a knowing, feeling, and thinking role', 'the physical heart', 'a living being's breath', 'a living being's emotions and feelings', 'the focus (of a thing)', and 'the centre
(of a place)' (author's translations/paraphrases). The order in which
the definitions are listed is noteworthy: the heart *qua* EPC is mentioned ahead of the "physical heart", which is sometimes referred
to as *hua chai* หัวใจ, lit. 'head of *chai*'. The same dictionary further

points out that *chai* can be used for the purpose of self-reference, in which case *chai* acts as the grammatical subject of a feeling, an emotion, or a thought (e.g. *chai krot* ใจโกรธ '*chai* is angry', hence 'I am angry'), or as a term of endearment (e.g. *duang chai* ดวงใจ 'a heart', where *duang* acts as a classifier).[3] All of these are further elaborated on with examples; however, in and by themselves the aforementioned paraphrases give a good initial impression of the word's current range of meanings, and help explain why the word *chai* is so commonly used in the Thai language. It is especially common in metaphorical compounds involving either verbs or adjectives.

Metaphorical *chai* expressions can be used to express a variety of mental and psychological states and processes, such as 'deliberating' (Example 1), 'showing sympathy' (Example 2), 'signalling preparedness' (Example 3), 'displaying interest' (Example 4), 'committing to memory' (Example 5), and 'paying attention' (Example 6).

1 พรสวรรค์อึ้งไปครู่หนึ่งคล้ายจะชั่งใจว่าควรพูดหรือไม่.

*Phonsawan ueng pai khrunueng khlai cha **chang chai** wa khuan phut ruemai.*

'Pornsawan was silent for a moment as if she was *weighing up* (lit. weighing *chai*) whether or not she should say it'.

(*Waeo Wan* 'The story of Waeo Wan' [fiction]; TNC)

2 คนที่เห็นภาพน้ำท่วม ก็คงมีความรู้สึกเห็นอกเห็นใจ สะเทือนใจ.

*Khon thi hen phap namthuam ko khong mi khwamrusuek **hen ok hen chai sathuean chai**.*

'Those who saw the flood photos will probably *sympathize* (lit. see a chest and *chai*) and *be deeply moved* (lit. *chai*-shaken)'.

(*Di Chan* [magazine]; TNC)

3 รวมแล้วลูกจ้างที่สมัครใจลาออกเองจะได้รับเงินไม่ต่ำกว่าคนละ 200,000 บาท.

*Ruam laeo lukchang thi **samak chai** la-ok eng cha dairap ngoen mai tam kwa khon la 200,000 bat.*

'Employees who are *willing* (lit. volunteering *chai*) to resign will each receive a total amount of money not less than 200,000 baht'.

(*Krungthep Turakit* [business newspaper]; TNC)

4 ขณะนั้นญี่ปุ่นสนใจดินแดนทางเอเชียตะวันออก เช่น จีน และเกาหลี มากกว่าที่จะสนใจทางแถบเอเชียตะวันออกเฉียงใต้ เช่น ไทย พม่า หรือลาว.

*Khananan yipun **son chai** dindaen thang echia tawan-ok chen chin lae kaoli mak kwa thi cha **son chai** thang thaep esia tawan-okchiangtai chen thai phama rue lao.*

'During that time, Japan *showed more interest* (lit. strung more *chai*) in East Asia, places like China and Korea, than in Southeast Asia, places like Thailand, Myanmar, or Laos'.

(*Prawattisat Yipun* 'Japanese history' [non-fiction]; TNC)

5 เลขหมายของเขาเธอจำได้ขึ้นใจ ไม่ต้องเสียเวลานึก.

*Lekmai khong khao thoe **cham dai khuen chai** mai tong sia wela nuke.*

'As for his phone number, she has *learned it by heart* (lit. remember in *chai*). She will have no difficulty recalling it'.

(*Thotlong Chai* 'Testing one's heart' [fiction]; TNC)

6 ไม่มีใครอีกแล้วในโลก ที่จะคอยฟังเธออย่างเอาใจใส่.

*Mai mi khrai ik laeo nai lok thi cha khoi fang thoe yang **ao chai sai.***

'No one else in this world will listen to her carefully and *attentively* (lit. taking *chai*) in her'.

(Ngan Sop Dokmai, *Ruam Bot Kawi* 'The funeral of flowers' [Collection of poetry]; TNC)

Living in a culture where feelings matter more than reason (Wichiarajote, 1984) and where emotions take centre stage, Thai speakers are especially likely to use metaphorical *chai* expressions to verbalize their feelings and emotions. They can form dozens of set or ad hoc phrases by combining the term *chai* with different types of adjectives. When *chai* is used as the second element of a compound, the result is a verb or adjective that describes a temporary feeling, as in Examples 7–9 (see also the second *chai* compound in Example 12):

7 ตื่นเช้าขึ้นมาแสนจะดีใจ ไม่ต้องไปโรงเรียน

*Tuen chao khuen ma saen cha **di chai** mai tong pai rongrian.*

'I woke up *happy* (lit. delighted *chai*), knowing that I did not have to go to school'.

(*Chiwit Nai Wang 1* 'Life inside the Palace, vol. 1' [non-fiction]; TNC)

8 แต่ยิ่งแม่บ่นว่าพ่อมากเท่าไร ฉันยิ่งเห็นใจพ่อมากเท่านั้น

*Tae ying mae bon wa pho mak thaorai chan ying **hen chai** pho mak thaonan.*

'The more mom complained to dad, the more I *sympathized* (lit. see *chai*) with him'.

(Ngan Sop Dokmai, *Ruam Bot Kawi* 'The funeral of flowers' [collection of poetry]; TNC)

9 มันอายเพื่อนที่เห็นพ่อขับรถไปส่ง บางครั้งเราก็น้อยใจ แต่ก็เข้าใจว่าลูกเป็นวัยรุ่นแล้ว

*Man ai phuean thi hen pho khaprot pai song bang khrang rao ko **noi chai** tae ko **khao chai** wa luk pen wairun laeo.*

'He was embarrassed around his friends that I drove him to school. Sometimes I *feel neglected* (lit. lessen *chai*) but then I *realize* (lit. enter into *chai*) that he's already a teenager'.

(Chusak Iamsuk, *Ha...Nong Ma Waeo* 'Nong is here: Life of a comedian' [non-fiction]; TNC)

When *chai* comes first, the result is an epithet describing the long-term nature or disposition of a person, as in Examples 10–12. Notice the use of *chai ron* ใจร้อน in Example 10 and of *ron chai* ร้อนใจ in Example 12: the former means 'hot-tempered' and is long-term, the latter means 'restless' and is short-term (but probably recurring).

10 เขาเป็นคนใจเย็น เราเป็นคนใจร้อน เราจะฟีบฟับๆ ต้องเสร็จแล้ว แต่เขาจะค่อยๆละเมียด

*Khao pen khon **chai yen**. Rao pen khon **chai ron**. Rao cha fuep fap fuep fap tong set laeo tae khao cha khoi khoi lamiat.*

'He's a *cool-headed* (lit. cool *chai*) person. I'm a *hot-tempered* (lit. hot *chai*) person. I'm always rushing to get things done while he does things slowly'.

(*Ploy Kaem Petch* [magazine]; TNC)

11 คุณแม่เป็นคนใจดีสมกับที่เป็นพยาบาล ไม่จู้จี้ขี้บ่นและใจกว้างมาก

*Khunmae pen khon **chai di** som kap thi pen phayaban. Mai chuchi khibon lae **chai kwang** mak.*

'Her mother is a *good-hearted* (lit. good *chai*) person, as expected of a nurse. She is not fussy and very *generous* (lit. spacious *chai*).

(Suwanna Kriengkraipetch, Chang Pa Ton Khon Suphan, 'Wild elephant in Suphanburi Province' [non-fiction]; TNC)

12 พลอยจำคำแม่ไว้ให้ดี ถ้าเจ้าจะมีลูกมีผัวต่อไปก็หาคนที่เขาใจเดียว อย่าไปได้ผัวเจ้าชู้เมียมาก จะต้องร้อนใจเหมือนแม่.

*Phloi cham kham mae wai hai di. Tha chao cha mi luk mi phua topai ko ha khon thi khao **chai diao**. Ya pai dai phua chaochu mia mak cha tong **ron chai** muean mae.*

'Ploy, you remember my word. If you're going to have a husband in the future, find someone who is *faithful* (lit. united *chai*). Do not get a husband who is flirtatious with many girls because you'll be *restless* (lit. heat up *chai*) like me, your mum'.

(Kukrit Pramoj, *Si Phaen Din* 'Four Reigns' [novel]; TNC)

Chai also occurs as a component in Thai moral values, such as *kreng chai* เกรงใจ 'fear of offending someone or causing trouble' (lit. awe for other *chai*), *kamlang chai* กำลังใจ 'moral support' (lit. strength of *chai*), or *nam chai* น้ำใจ 'thoughtfulness' (lit. water of *chai*). These are illustrated in Examples 13–15.

13 ในที่สุดเราสองคนก็ตกลงยอมดูลายมือตรวจโชคชะตาราศีเนื่องจาก รู้สึกเกรงใจหมอดู ตามประสาคนไทยขี้ใจอ่อนทั้งหลาย.

*Nai thisut rao song khon ko toklong yom du laimue truat chokchata rasi nueangchak rusuek **kreng chai** modu tam pra sa khon thai **khi chai on** thanglai.*

'We eventually decided to have our palms checked for the future for we were *afraid of offending* the fortune-teller, like other Thai people with a *submissive* nature (lit. soft *chai*)'.

(Kukrit Pramoj, *Si Phaen Din* 'Four Reigns' [novel]; TNC)

14 ขอเป็นกำลังใจให้พี่ๆ ทุกคน ช่วยกันสร้างสรรค์สิ่งดีๆ ให้กับสังคม
ไทยต่อไปครับ

*Kho pen **kamlang chai** hai phiphi thuk khon chuai kan sangsan
sing didi hai kap sangkhom thai to pai khrap*

'I would like to offer *moral support* to all of you to continue
creating good things for Thai society'.

(Reader's letter in *Kho Khon* [magazine]; TNC)

15 ชนนก็อาสาอย่างมีน้ำใจ พี่ไปส่งให้ดีไหม

*Chanon ko asa yang mi **nam chai**. Phi pai song hai di mai.*

'Chanon made a *thoughtful* offer. Would you like a ride?'

(*A Better Man … Roi Yim Khong Chaochai Nitra* 'A better
man … A smile from a slumbering prince' [fiction]; TNC)

In addition, as per the information contained in the dictionary referred to at the beginning of this section, *chai* is occasionally used to
replace the first-person pronoun, especially in the structure '*chai* +
free morpheme', where it acts as the grammatical subject of a feeling,
an emotion, or a thought. Thus, *chai chep* ใจเจ็บ literally means '*chai*
is painful', hence 'I am hurt'. Used on its own, *chai* ใจ also often explicitly refers to one of the two parts of a human being (and of other
creatures), demonstrating dualism between *chai* ใจ and *kai* กาย
'body'. This is particularly so in the popular saying *Chai pen nai, Kai
pen bao* ใจเป็นนาย กายเป็นบ่าว '*Chai* is the master, Body the servant'.

All of these are well-known uses of *chai*, but they do not exhaust
the list. The younger generations in particular often coin new
words and slang expressions that are not listed in standard dictionaries but are instead tailored to the specific circumstances in
which they arise. There is more than a reasonable chance that they
will call upon the word *chai* to express hard-to-verbalize psychological and mental experiences, and to translate into language the
idiosyncratic feelings they experience at the spur of the moment.
Examples are common in the social media, other online outlets,
and song lyrics:

16 ทริปล้างใจ จะช่วยได้มั๊ยนะ.

*Thrip **lang chai** cha chuai dai mai na.*

'Would a trip to *revive our lost feelings* (lit. wash *chai*) help?'

(Amazing Thailand [Facebook], June 2017)

17 เงิน กับ ความรัก : ทำไมคุณผู้ชายไม่"ใจ"เลยอ่ะคะ.

*Ngoen kap khwam rak thammai khun phuchai **mai "chai"** loei a ka.*

'Between money and love: Why men are *not dedicated* (lit. not *chai*)?'

(pantip.com [online discussion forum], March 2014)

18 เฉลิมชัยร่อนจดหมายเคลียร์ใจ ยันดีใจล้มเลิกระบบรับน้องแบบเก่าๆ.

*Chaloem chai ron chotmai **khlia chai**. Yan dichai lomloek rabop rap nong baep kao kao.*

'Chalermchai sent out a letter to *clarify his thoughts/feelings and resolve the conflict* (lit. clear *chai*). He insisted that he was happy to see the old system of university hazing rituals abolished'.

(*Matichon* [online newspaper], September 2017)

19 ก็เลยมาร้องเพลงบอก แค่อยากให้เธอนั้นเข้าใจ ไอ้สิ่งที่ฉันทำลงไป ใจสั่งมา.

*Ko loei ma rongphleng bok khae yak hai thoe nan **khao chai** ai sing thi chan tham long pai **chai sang ma**.*

'So I sing this song to you, begging you to *understand* (lit. enter into *chai*) that all I did was *follow the command of my heart* (lit. *chai* ordered me)'.

(*Chai Sang Ma* 'The command of my heart' [Song lyric], October 1999)

Of the two instances of *chai* in Example 19, the first is well established and was already illustrated in Example 9; the second is the innovative one.

In conclusion, there is plenty of evidence to suggest that *chai*, in modern Thai, has become a highly versatile word that can be used in its own right, as a noun, or in a variety of compound nouns, verbs, adjectives, and even adverbs. Its precise grammatical status can at times be problematic. *Chai* demonstrates high flexibility in a relatively free linguistic form. Section 3 is aimed at showing how this came about.

3 Semantic Development of *Chai* ใจ

Chai ใจ is believed to derive from a Proto-Thai word that originally meant 'breath' (Diller & Juntanamalaga, 1990). This is still a possible meaning of *chai* today, as pointed out at the start of Section 2.

In Modern Thai, the compound *hai chai* หายใจ means 'to breathe' (lit. recover *chai*), and health professionals today recommend *hai chai* หายใจ 'breathing' as the simplest way to relieve stress. But *chai* is not attested in that reconstructed meaning in the oldest Thai texts. Subsections 3.1–3.3 investigate the historical development of the word throughout the Sukhothai, Ayutthaya, and Rattanakosin periods, each of which coincides with a dynasty that goes by the same name.[4]

3.1 The Sukhothai Period (1238–1438)

The Sukhothai period is named after the Sukhothai Kingdom, located in the area around the city of Sukhothai in lower Northern Thailand. The kingdom existed from 1238 until around 1438, when a gradual merger with the Ayutthaya Kingdom commenced. The word *chai* first appears as early as the end of the 13th century, in the oldest surviving ancient Siamese inscription, on the King Ram Khamhaeng stele or *Sila Charuek Lak Thi Nueng* (1292).[5] Three appearances of the word *chai* are found in it.[6] On Face 1 of the stele, *chai* is the 'locus' where a certain psychological activity occurs, analogous to a sickening feeling occurring in a physical part of the body, such as the belly. The compound *khong chai* ของใจ literally means 'to have something trapped in one's *chai*'.

20   ปากประตูมีกะดิ่งอันถ่ึงแขวนไว้หั้นไพร่ฟ้าหน้าปก กลางบ้านกลางเมือง
มีถ้อยมีความเจ็บท้องข้องใจ มันจักกล่าวเถิงเจ้าเถิง ขุนบ่ไร้ ไปลั่นกะ –
ดิ่งอันท่านแขวนไว้ พ่อขุนรามคำแหงเจ้าเมืองได้

*Pak pratu mi ka ding an nueng khwaen wai han phraifa na pok klangban klangmueang. Mi thoi mi khwam chep thong **khong chai**, man chak klao thoeng chao thoeng khun bo rai; pai lan ka ding an than khwaen wai phokhun ram kham ngae chao mueang dai.*

'He [the King] has hung a bell in the opening of the gate over there. If any commoner in the land has a grievance that sickens their belly and *gripes their heart*, and that they want to make known to their ruler and lord, it is easy: they go and strike the bell the King has hung there'.

(Face 1 of the King Ram Khamhaeng stele, Lines 32–35)

On Face 4 of the stele, the word *chai* occurs twice in the phrase *ha khrai chai nai chai* หาใคร่ใจในใจ. The old Thai word *ha* หา means 'by oneself', *khrai chai* ใคร่ใจ means 'to have one's *chai* set on something', and *nai chai* ในใจ means 'in one's *chai*'. This compelling statement serves as the stele's highlight since it offers significant evidence that the modern Thai alphabet originated with King Ram Khamhaeng in the year 1283.

21 ๑๒๐๕ ศกปีมะแม พ่อขุนรามคำแหง หาใคร่ใจ ในใจ แลใส่ลายสือ ไทยนี้ ลายสือไทนี้จึงมีเพื่อขุนผู้นั้นใส่ไว้

*1205 sok pi mamae phokhun ram kham ngae **ha khrai chai nai chai** lae sai lai sue thai ni. Lai sue thai ni chueng mi phuea khun phu nan sai wai.*

'In 1205 Saka, a Year of the Goat [AD 1283], King Ram Khamhaeng *set his intention* (lit. set in *chai*) on devising these Tai letters. So these Tai letters exist thanks to him'.

(Face 4 of the King Ram Khamhaeng stele, Lines 9–11)

Many more occurrences of *chai* are found in the oldest preserved text of Thai Buddhist literature, *Traiphum Phra Ruang* 'Three worlds according to King Ruang', written by Phya Lithai in 1345. There are over 300 instances of *chai* appearing in this work, which portrays a Thai Buddhist cosmology centred on the concept of *chai*, with a focus on the description of good and bad deeds as well as on the fates awaiting those who committed them, fates that varied according to each individual's karma. Here, *chai* is used to refer to a person's disposition (e.g. *chai di* ใจดี 'good *chai*', *chai trong* ใจตรง 'upright/honest *chai*'), as well as to indicate moral judgement (e.g. *thambap duai chai an rai* ทำบาปด้วยใจอันร้าย 'do evil deeds with a wicked *chai*'). Two examples are shown in the following.[7]

22 เพราะเขาเห็นท่านนั้นมีรูปโฉมอันงามกว่าคนทั้งหลาย แล้รู้ว่าคนทั้ง หลายแลใจงาม ใจดีกว่าคนทั้งหลาย ใจซื่อ ใจตรง ใจบุญ ยิ่งกว่าคนทั้ง หลาย เขาเห็นดังนั้นเขาจึงตั้งให้เป็นพระญา เป็นเจ้าเป็นจอมเขา

*Phro khao hen than nan mi rup chom an ngam kwa khon thanglai lae ru kwa khon thanglai lae **chai ngam chai di** kwa khon thanglai **chai sue chai trong chai bui** ying kwa khon thanglai. Khao hen dangnan khao chueng tang hai pen phra ya pen chao pen chom khao.*

'Because they think you are more beautiful and intellectual than others, having a more *beautiful heart* (lit. beautiful *chai*), *good heart* (lit. good *chai*), *faithful heart* (lit. honest *chai*), *upright heart* (lit. upright *chai*), *benevolent heart* (lit. virtuous *chai*) than others. That is why they agree to appoint you as the leader'.

23 ฝูงสัตว์อันไปเกิดในที่ร้ายที่เป็นทุกขลำบากใจเขานั้นเพื่อใจเขาร้าย
    และทำบาปด้วยใจอันร้ายมี ๑๒ อันแลฯ

*Fung sat an pai koet nai thi rai thi pen thukkha lambak **chai** khao nan phuea **chai** khao rai lae thambap duai **chai** an rai mi 12 an lae.*

'Certain beings are born in evil places where they have *mental difficulties* (lit. suffering and troubled *chai*), because their *chai* is evil, and with this wicked *chai* they do evil deeds. There are twelve kinds of such evil states of *chai*'.[8]

3.2 The Ayutthaya Period (1350–1767)

When the power of the Sukhothai Kingdom began to fade towards the end of the 14th century, King Ramathibodi I or King U-thong, the first king of the Ayutthaya Kingdom established his own capital in the new city of Ayutthaya, located in Central Thailand, and successfully took control of the Sukhothai Kingdom in the mid-15th century.

Ayutthaya literary works suggest that *chai* takes on a broader meaning: no longer confined to its primitive use as a fixed or static entity of intellectual, spiritual, and psychological activities, it acquires a new, more cognitive use as a floating dynamic. *Lilit Phra Lo* 'The tale of King Phra Lo', one of the best-known Thai literary works, written in the early Ayutthaya period, has a large number of metaphorical *chai* expressions that are still widely used nowadays. Thought to have been written between 1448 and 1483, it was commended as the best Thai verse by King Rama VI's *Wannakhadi Samoson* (the Thai Royal Literary Club) in 1916. It depicts the tragic love story of King Phra Lo and the two princess sisters of a rival kingdom, who all die together when the King's mother seeks revenge for the death of her husband (the previous king) in a war between the kingdoms. There are more than 200 occurrences of *chai* found in this text. Some are reminiscent of earlier use in the Sukhothai period, e.g. *chai than* ใจธรรม 'virtuous *chai*', *lo laolom chai* ล่อเล้าโลมใจ 'consoling *chai*', *chai thao tha fuean fan* ใจท้าวธเฟือนฟั้น 'his *chai* is frantic', and *nap yu nai chai* นับอยู่ในใจ 'count in one's *chai*'. Some are used in a more innovative way, as terms of endearment, e.g. *chom chai* จอมใจ 'sweetheart' (lit. top of *chai*), *chai kaeo* ใจแก้ว 'beloved *chai*', and *kloi chai* กลอยใจ 'united *chai*'. The majority of instances appear either in the form of conceptual metaphorical compounds or of phrasal compounds. More examples of *chai* compounds in *Lilit Phra Lo* may be found in Appendix A.

In addition to the previous examples, there are also some other metaphorical uses of *chai* that extend from its original meaning in the Sukhothai period. *Chai* comes to refer to the centre of something in phrases such as *chai lok* ใจโลก 'centre of the world' and *chai mueang* ใจเมือง 'centre of the city'; to a person's 'breath' or 'life', as in *klan chai tai* กลั้นใจตาย 'hold one's breath to die', and *chai cha khat ron ron* ใจจะขาดรอนรอน '*chai* is going to tear apart'; as well as to Thai social and cultural values, as in *nam chai* น้ำใจ 'thoughtfulness', *kreng chai* เกรงใจ 'deference', and *khop chai* ขอบใจ 'return *chai*', which will later become the common expression for 'Thank you'.

24 ชมข่าวสองพี่น้อง ต้องหฤทัยจอมราช พระบาทให้รางวัล ปันผ้าเสื้อ สนอบ ขอบใจสู่เอาข่าว มากล่าวต้องติดใจ บารนี ฯ

> *Chom khao songphinong tong haruethai chom rat phrabat hai rangwan pan pha suea sanop **khop chai** su ao khao ma klao tong titchai barani.*

'King Lo thanked (lit. returned *chai* to) the person who brought the news about the beauty of the two princess sisters and rewarded him with royal clothing'.

(*Lilit Phra Lo* 'The tale of King Phra Lo')

Chai is occasionally employed in compounds that bring together, and implicitly contrast, the two parts of a person (body and *chai*), e.g. *chai nueai* ใจเหนื่อย '*chai* exhaustion' (hence downheartedness), *khai chai* ไข้ใจ '*chai* fever' (i.e. lovesickness):

25 ผิวไข้พูลพยาธิไซร้ ยาหาย ง่ายนา
    ไข้หลากทั้งหลายใคร ช่วยได้
    ไข้ใจแต่จักตาย ดีกว่า ไส้นา
    สองพี่นึกในไว้ แต่ถ้าเผาเผือ ฯ

> *Phiwa khai phun phayat sai ya hai ngai na*
> *Khai lak thanglai khrai chuai dai*
> ***Khai chai** tae chak tai di kwa sai na*
> *Song phi nuek nai wai tae tha phao phuea*

'A (physical) fever is easy to cure,
there are many who can help.
A *chai fever* is different, it is better to die.
The two sisters ponder'.

(*Lilit Phra Lo* 'The tale of King Phra Lo')

The word *chai* makes repeated appearances in a variety of literary texts of the late Ayutthaya period. Example 26, from *Phra Malai Khamluang* 'The legend of Phra Malai' (1737), demonstrates the use of *chai* to denote a person's disposition. Example 27, from *Khlong Nirat Chaofa Aphai* 'Nirat poetry of Prince Apai' (date of composition unknown), represents *chai* as the seat of feelings, analogous to the use observed in the Sukhothai period.

26 อกุศลต้อนเตือนแต่ง อายุแห่งสัตว์น้อย เดิมขับร้อยถอยถด ลำดับลด
หลนลง ร้อยขวบคงสิบปี ห้าขวบมีฆราวาส ใจร้ายกาจโลกี กัลปนั้นมี
นามกร ชื่อว่าสัตถันดร พึงมี

*Akuson ton tuean taeng. Ayu haeng sat noi. Doem khap roi
thoithot. Lamdap lot lon long. Roi khuap khong sip pi. Ha khuap
mi kharawat. **Chai** raikat lo ki. Kanlapa nan mi nammakon.
Chuewa sattathandon phueng mi.*

'The accumulated sin will shorten a life span from a hundred years to ten. Some will start to have a spouse from as early as 5 years old. People's *chai* will turn evil. That age is called *Sattathandon*'.

(*Phra Malai Khamluang* 'The legend of Phra Malai')

27 เห็นวังวาริศร้าง ริมแคว น้ำนา
พระนครหลวงแล เปล่าเศร้า
วังราชฤๅมาแปร เปนป่า
เกรงจะแปรใจเจ้า ห่างแล้วลืมเรียม

*Hen wang wari sang rim khwae nam na
Phra nakhon luang lae plao sao
Wang ratcharue ma prae pen pa
Kreng cha prae **chai** chao hang laeo luem riam.*

'The spectacle of the deserted palace by the river
gives the capital a sense of loneliness.
The palace has changed into a forest.
I am worried your *chai*, too, will change and forget me while I am away'.

(*Khlong Nirat Chaofa Aphai* 'Nirat Poetry of Prince Apai')

3.3 The Rattanakosin Period (1782–Present)

The Rattanakosin Kingdom was founded in 1782 on the island of Rattanakosin, and Bangkok established as its capital city. King Rama I, the first ruler of the kingdom, was also the founder of the Chakri Dynasty, the current ruling dynasty of Thailand.

During the Rattanakosin period, *chai* becomes one of the most frequently used words of the Thai language. In this period, *chai* refers to a solid entity representing a person's disposition as well as a locus where feelings and thoughts are perceived. The increased use of *chai* in metaphorical compounds and idioms is the most notable change from earlier periods. *Chai* is used more often and in a wider range of expressions, including those representing intellectual capabilities, such as *chai chalat* ใจฉลาด 'a clever *chai*'.

There are more than 2,000 occurrences of *chai* in the script of the *Ramakien* play, the Thai national epic based on the well-known Hindu *Ramayana*. The play's script was compiled between 1799 and 1807 under the supervision of King Rama I. Examples 28 and 29 illustrate two metaphorical compounds: *tok chai* ตกใจ 'to be frightened' and *plong chai* ปลงใจ 'to make a decision':

28 เมื่อนั้น ทศเศียรสุริยวงศ์รังสรรค์
     เห็นน้องท้าวเจ็บปวดจาบัลย์ กุมภัณฑ์ตระหนกตกใจ

     Mueanan thotsasian suriyawong rangsan
     Hen nong thao cheppuat chaban kumphan tranok **tok chai.**

     'The 10-faced demon *took fright* (lit. dropped down *chai*) at the sight of his severely wounded brother'.

     (*Ramakien* 'Glory of Rama', King Rama I's version)

29 เอาภูษาผูกศอให้มั่น แล้วพันกับกิ่งโศกใหญ่
     หลับเนตรดำรงปลงใจ อรไทก็โจนลงมา

     Ao phusa phuk so hai man laeo phan kap king sok yai
     Lap net damrong **plong chai** *orathai ko chon long ma.*

     'Sida [Lord Rama's consort] tied a piece of cloth firmly around her neck and strung it to a large tree branch. She closed her eyes and *decided to* (lit. lay down *chai*) jump'.

     (*Ramakien* 'Glory of Rama', King Rama I's version)

During the reign of King Rama II, known as the Golden Age of Thai Literature, *chai* will be employed extensively in more than 30 literary works, mostly written in verse form by a number of famous poets at the royal court, including the King himself. Consider Examples 30–33:

30 ยำใหญ่ใส่สารพัด วางจานจัดหลายเหลือตรา
     รสดีด้วยน้ำปลา ญี่ปุ่นล้ำย้ำยวนใจ

Yam yai sai saraphat wang chan chat lai luea tra
*Rot di duai nampla yipun lam yam **yuan chai**.*

'Yum Yai [a spicy Thai salad] can be arranged in many styles with a variety of ingredients. It is flavoured with Japanese fish sauce (shoyu), which produces an *appealing taste* (lit. seduces *chai*)'.

(*Kap He Ruea Chom Khrueang Khao Wan* 'Culinary poetry of King Rama II')

31 เมื่อนั้น นางมณฑาหนวกหูอยู่ไม่ได้
ลุกเดินออกมาว่าอะไร ไม่เกรงเนื้อเกรงใจผู้ใหญ่เลย

Mueanan nang montha nuakhu yu mai dai
*Luk doen ok ma wa arai mai **kreng nuea kreng chai** phuyai loei.*

'It became so noisy that Montha [the mother of Princess Rodjana and her six sisters] could no longer bear it. She came out and reproached her daughters that they did not have deference towards the adults (lit. were not in awe of the flesh and *chai* of others)'.

(*Sang Thong* 'Tale of the conch-shell prince')

32 คนใดใจฉลาดด้วย ปัญญา
ฟังนักปราชญ์จรรจา ทั่วผู้
แจ้งธรรมบัดเดี๋ยวมา พลันทราบ ใจนา
ดุจดั่งลิ้นอันรู้ ทราบด้วยรสแกง

*Khon dai **chai chalat** duai panya*
Fang nakprat chancha thua phu
Chaeng tham batdiao ma phlan sap chai na
Dut dang lin an ru sap duai rot kaeng.

'Anybody who *is clever* (lit. whose *chai* is clever) by wisdom will be able to understand at once what philosophers say, just like when a tongue tastes soup'.

(*Khlong lokkanit* 'Lokkanit Didactic Poetry')

33 จะว่าเนื่องตามเรื่องนิยายพลัน ท่านผู้ฟังทั้งนั้นจงเข้าใจ

Cha wa nueang tam rueang niyai phlan than phufang thangnan
*chong **khao chai**.*

'I will now tell a story according to the folklore, hoping that the audience will *comprehend* (lit. enter into *chai*)'.

(*Khun Chang Khun Phaen* '[The triangle love story of] Khun Chang and Khun Phaen')

Chai phrasal compounds and idioms are increasingly used in a cognitive sense, including expressions involving intellectual capabilities, such as 'to make up one's mind', 'to understand', or 'to be clever' (see Examples 32 and 33). This is an expansion into a wider range of use; meanwhile, the word *chai* continues to maintain its original meaning in other contexts. It plays an important part in literary prose, which has become more common since the reign of King Rama V, an era of domestic reforms and modernization brought about by the threat of Western colonialism. The high frequency and wider scope of *chai* ใจ usage are evident in one of the better-known literary works, *Klai Ban* 'Far from home', a compilation of 43 personal letters written by the King himself to his Queen and daughters when he visited England and various European countries (originally published in 1907). In the first letter (containing no less than 5,720 words), there are 37 occurrences of *chai*, i.e. one occurrence on average in every 154 words. Examples 34–42 illustrate how the King used the word in context:

34 แต่มีการร้องไห้กันเสียนุงนังจนใจทรึมเต็มที

   *Tae mi kan ronghai kan sia nungnang chon **chai suem** temthi.*

   'There were many people crying and that makes my *heart* become so *gloomy* (lit. *chai* is gloomy)'.

35 ตกลงเปนอันไม่ร่ำคาญใจนัก

   *Toklong pen an mai **ramkhan chai** nak.*

   'So it was not that *annoying* (lit. annoy *chai*)'.

36 รู้สึกเปลี่ยวใจวังเวงใจกลับไปบ้าน

   Rusuek pliao chai wangweng chai klap pai ban.

   'I felt so lonely (lit. desolate *chai*) that I wanted to go home'.

37 กับเข้าฝรั่งเขาก็จัดดี กับเข้าไทยก็บริบูรณ์ ไม่ได้มีความอดอยากเลย อยากอะไรได้ดังใจ พ่อกินเข้าได้เสมอทุกวัน

   *Kap khao farang khao ko chat di. Kap khao thai ko boribun mai dai mi khwam-otyak loei. Yak arai dai **dang chai**. Pho kin khao dai samoe thuk wan.*

   'Western-style food is well arranged and there is plenty of Thai food. Not a chance to starve. I get everything *as I wish* (lit. as *chai* wishes). I can eat well every day'.

38   เซอยอนแอนเดอซัน กิริยาอัชฌาไศรยเรียบร้อย พูดจาด้วยสบายใจดี

*Soe yon aendoesan kiriya atcha sai riaproi. Phutcha duai **sabai chai** di.*

'Sir Anderson has a polite manner. It was *a pleasure* (lit. comfort *chai*) speaking with him'.

39   จะให้ออกเรือเมื่อไรก็ได้ แต่เราจะต้องเกรงใจเขา

*Cha hai-ok ruea muearai kodai tae rao cha tong **kreng chai** khao.*

'We can order the ship to depart at any time but we have to *be considerate* (lit. be in awe of their *chai*)'.

40   เมื่อแรกเห็นเรือเบอม่า เอามาผูกใจนึกว่ามันจะอัดแอไม่สบาย

*Muea raek hen ruea boe ma ao ma **phuk chai** nuek wa man cha at-ae mai sabai.*

'When I first saw the Burmese ship, I *presumed* (lit. tied with *chai*) that it would be crowded and uncomfortable'.

41   ใจคอมันให้ระส่ำระสายอีกเปนครั้งที่สอง

***Chai kho** man hai rasamrasai ik pen khrang thi song.*

'I felt anxious (lit. had *chai* and neck being in a state of disunity) again for the second time'.

42   แต่ที่ห่างจะห่างแต่กาย ใจคงจะผูกพันกลับไปบ้านทุกวัน วันละหลายหน

*Tae thi hang cha hang tae kai. **Chai** khong cha phukphan klap pai ban thuk wan. Wan la lai hon.*

'I am only away with respect to my body parts. My *heart* (lit. *chai*) is bound with home, going back many times a day and every day'.

After the reign of King Rama V, *chai* continues its spread into works of prose, both fiction and non-fiction, produced by Kings, nobles, royal clerks, and also by the general population. Appendix B shows some examples of *chai* compounds during this period. It is also worth noting that there are two types of syntactic structures depending on the position of *chai* in the compound: (1) *chai* + free morpheme and (2) free morpheme + *chai*. The former structure, found in the older use of the word, is primarily that of an adjective or a noun referring to a relatively permanent state or disposition of a person. The latter, on the other hand, functions as a verb, representing a temporary psychological state or temporary mental behaviour, which gains in frequency in the Ayutthaya period.

4 *Chai* ใจ: An Explication in NSM (English and Thai)

A sophisticated descriptive tool is needed to explicate the meaning of individual EPCs and to tease out differences between them. This chapter, like all others in this volume, employs the NSM approach as a methodological framework for semantic analysis to avoid ethnocentrism and cultural bias. It relies on the current, thought-to-be near-final, list of 65 semantic primes and their combinatorial properties and proposes both an English and a Thai version of the explication of the word *chai* ใจ in the Thai language.

What would or could an NSM explication of *chai* look like? The one that follows is a significantly amended version of a previous attempt (Svetanant, 2013) based on work in progress by the Danish linguist Carsten Levisen. It used a template consisting of four parts:

a   a *partonymic* part, which deals with the general status of the EPC in relation to the entire person;
b   a *characteristics* part, which deals with the typical features or nature of the EPC;
c   a *dynamics* part, which deals with the working and functions of the EPC;
d   an *evaluation* part, which deals with what is perceived as "good" or "bad" in relation to the EPC.

Levisen's proposal for an EPC template was not published until 2017, by which time it had different labels for two of the four parts, which he refers to as *General conceptual status, Characteristics, Dynamics,* and *Social valuation.* The first three parts are fixed; the fourth is optional in that it may be required for some EPCs but not for others. In what follows, I adopt Levisen's (2017) labels and print them, as he does, on the right of the first line of each clause. I do not need the *Social valuation* part, but I do add a new part called *Control.*

4.1 General Conceptual Status

There is concrete evidence that, used on its own, *chai* often explicitly refers to one of the two parts of a human being (and indeed of other creatures), demonstrating dualism between *chai* ใจ and *kai* กาย 'body'. As mentioned in Section 2, this is particularly so in the popular saying *chai pen nai, kai pen bao* ใจเป็นนาย กายเป็นบ่าว '*chai* is the master, body the servant'. The dualism is also quite clear in expressions such as *kreng nuea kreng chai* เกรงเนื้อเกรงใจ 'be in awe of flesh and *chai* of others' (which includes a direct reference to the Thai cultural value *kreng chai* เกรงใจ, also referred to in Section 2), *hen ok hen chai* เห็นอกเห็นใจ 'sympathize' (lit. see a chest and *chai*), *mai lambak kai tae lambak chai* ไม่ลำบากกายแต่ลำบากใจ 'be in psychological trouble, not physical trouble', and *hang kai tae mai hang chai* ห่างกายแต่ไม่ห่างใจ 'physically far away but mentally close'.

In addition (this, too, was mentioned in Section 2, in the glossed dictionary entry at the start), *chai* is occasionally used to replace the first-person pronoun, especially in the structure '*chai* + free morpheme', where *chai* acts as the grammatical subject of a feeling, an emotion, or a thought. *Chai chep* ใจเจ็บ literally means '*chai* is painful', hence 'I am hurt'; likewise for *chai krot* ใจโกรธ '*chai* is angry', *chai due* ใจดื้อ '*chai* is stubborn', *chai ramkhan* ใจรำคาญ '*chai* is annoyed', *chai awon* ใจอาวรณ์ '*chai* is concerned about', *chai rak* ใจรัก '*chai* loves', **chai** *ko khit wa yang nan* ใจก็คิดว่าอย่างนั้น '*chai* thinks so', etc. In these examples, a part of someone (someone's *chai*) is extended and applies to the entire person; this, too, could be seen as evidence of dualism since the entire person obviously consists of that person's body and of their *chai*.

Finally, of the two parts of a person, as conceptualized in Thai, only the body is visible; *chai* is the other, invisible part. With this in mind, I propose the following content for the *General conceptual status* block of my explication. The explication itself is anthropocentric and is for "someone's" *chai*; this justifies the reference to "this someone" in the first line. The fact that *chai* is thought of as a part of not only human beings but, more broadly, all living things is acknowledged at the end.

something inside this someone   GENERAL CONCEPTUAL STATUS

this something is one of two parts of this someone

the other part is this someone's body

this part is not a part of this someone's body

this part is somewhere inside the left of the upper part of this someone's body

people cannot see this part

all people have this part

at the same time, it is like this: all living things have this part

บางสิ่งข้างในคนคนนี้   GENERAL CONCEPTUAL STATUS

บางสิ่งนี้เป็นหนึ่งในสองส่วนของคนคนนี้

ส่วนอื่นคือร่างกายของคนคนนี้

ส่วนนี้ไม่ใช่ส่วนของร่างกายคนคนนี้

ส่วนนี้อยู่ในที่แห่งหนึ่งข้างในส่วนบนซ้ายของร่างกายคนคนนี้

คนไม่สามารถเห็นส่วนนี้

คนทั้งหมดมีส่วนนี้

ในเวลาเดียวกัน, มันเป็นอย่างนี้: สิ่งมีชีวิตทั้งหมดมีส่วนนี้

4.2 Characteristics

The second block of the explication deals with the characteristics of *chai*. As we have seen, a variety of mental and psychological states and processes can be described by means of common and widely used *chai* phrases, some of which were exemplified in Section 2 (Examples 1–6). More generally, the states and processes identified by means of *chai* phrases include:

- thoughts, deliberations, and decisions: e.g. *sathon chai* สะท้อนใจ 'reflect' (lit. reflect in *chai*), *chang chai* ชั่งใจ 'weigh up, deliberate' (lit. weigh *chai*), *tatsin chai* ตัดสินใจ 'decide' (lit. decide *chai*);
- expressions of sympathy and mercy: e.g. *hen chai* เห็นใจ 'sympathize' (lit. see *chai*), *sathuean chai* สะเทือนใจ 'be deeply moved' (lit. shake *chai*);
- expressions of intention and will: e.g. *tang chai* ตั้งใจ 'intend' (lit. set up *chai*), *samak chai* สมัครใจ 'be willing to' (lit. volunteer *chai*);
- expressions of trust, interest, or enthusiasm: e.g. *chuea chai* เชื่อใจ 'trust' (lit. believe in *chai*), *son chai* สนใจ 'take an interest in' (lit. string *chai*), *tit chai* ติดใจ 'fascinate' (lit. stick to *chai*);
- intellectual activities, including memories: e.g. *khao chai* เข้าใจ 'understand' (lit. enter into *chai*), *cham khuen chai* จำขึ้นใจ 'memorize' (lit. remember in *chai*)
- references to attention and caution: e.g. *ao chai sai* เอาใจใส่ 'be attentive, pay attention to' (lit. take *chai* in), *chuk chai* ฉุกใจ 'have an inkling' (lit. suddenly occur to *chai*).

All of these can be spelled out in terms of living, knowing, feeling, and thinking:

because someone has this part, it is like this:	CHARACTERISTICS
this someone can live	
this someone can know many things	
this someone can think many things	
this someone can feel many things	

เพราะคนคนหนึ่งมีส่วนนี้, มันเป็นอย่างนี้:	CHARACTERISTICS
คนคนนี้สามารถมีชีวิตอยู่	
คนคนนี้สามารถรู้หลายสิ่ง	
คนคนนี้สามารถคิดหลายสิ่ง	
คนคนนี้สามารถรู้สึกหลายสิ่ง	

4.3 Dynamics

In terms of its dynamics, which is what the third block of the explication sets out to capture, *chai* is highly sensitive to change, depending on the mental or psychological activity it gets involved in. *Chai* is warm and cool when things are under control, but it can become hot and cold when they are not. *Chai* can temporarily change in terms of its shape, size, colour, and temperature. In general, when *chai* encounters a pleasant or virtuous experience, it becomes spacious, high, light, bright, and fluffy. On the contrary, when it encounters an undesirable or vicious experience, it will become narrow, low, heavy, dark, and rough. Dozens of set or ad hoc phrases obtained by combining the term *chai* with different types of adjectives bear witness to this.

One type expresses physical states and dimensions: *on* อ่อน 'soft', *khaeng* แข็ง 'hard', *nak* หนัก 'heavy', *bao* เบา 'light', *kwang* กว้าง 'spacious', *khaep* แคบ 'narrow', etc. Another type refers to sensations or to emotional states; examples include *ron* ร้อน 'hot', *yen* เย็น 'cold', *un* อุ่น 'warm', *sabai* สบาย 'comfortable', *chep* เจ็บ 'painful', *sao* เศร้า 'sad', *nueai* เหนื่อย 'exhausted', and *ngao* เหงา 'lonely'. A third type belongs to the moral and evaluative realm, e.g. *bun* บุญ 'meritorious', *bap* บาป 'sinful', *di* ดี 'good', *chua* ชั่ว 'bad', *borisut* บริสุทธิ์ 'pure', *sokkaprok* สกปรก 'dirty', *ngam* งาม 'beautiful', *naknaen* หนักแน่น 'firm', *khlat* ขลาด 'cowardly', and *kla* กล้า 'fearless'.

The same forms often act as verbs: thus, *un* อุ่น can also mean 'warm up', *ron* ร้อน 'heat up, boil', etc.

When *chai* is used as the second element of a compound, the result is a verb or adjective that describes a temporary feeling. This was illustrated in Section 2, by means of Examples 7–9. The following is a more complete (but by no means exhaustive) list of possible combinations: *un chai* อุ่นใจ '(be) relieved' (lit. warm up *chai*), *ron chai* ร้อนใจ '(be) anxious, restless' (lit. heat up *chai*), *kin chai* กินใจ '(be) impressed, (be) doubtful' (lit. eat *chai*), *sia chai* เสียใจ '(be) sad' (lit. lose *chai*), *tok chai* ตกใจ '(be) startled' (lit. drop *chai*), *di chai* ดีใจ '(be) glad, happy' (lit. delighted *chai*), *nueai chai* เหนื่อยใจ '(be) downhearted, (be) mentally exhausted' (lit. exhausted *chai*), *ngao chai* เหงาใจ '(be) lonely' (lit. lonely *chai*), *hen chai* เห็นใจ 'sympathize, sympathetic' (lit. see *chai*), *noi chai* น้อยใจ 'feel neglected' (lit. lessen *chai*), *khao chai* เข้าใจ 'understand' (lit. enter into *chai*).

When *chai* comes first, the result is an epithet describing the long-term nature or disposition of a person. This, too, was illustrated in Section 2 by means of Examples 10–12. A more complete (but again by no means exhaustive) list of possible combinations includes: *chai di* ใจดี 'good-hearted' (lit. good *chai*), *chai bun* ใจบุญ 'kind-hearted' (lit. virtuous *chai*), *chai bap* ใจบาป 'wicked' (lit. sinful *chai*), *chai naknaen* ใจหนักแน่น 'constant, determined' (lit. firm *chai*), *chai ron* ใจร้อน 'hot-tempered' (lit. hot *chai*), *chai yen* ใจเย็น 'cool-headed' (lit. cool *chai*), *chai kwang* ใจกว้าง 'generous' (lit. spacious *chai*), *chai khaep* ใจแคบ 'narrow-minded' (lit. narrow *chai*), and *chai diao* ใจเดียว 'single-minded, faithful' (lit. united *chai*).

Not only is *chai* prone to change; it can also move around the body, up and down, and in and out, according to the emotions or the thoughts of the moment. At the same time, a person's *chai* is their innermost secret part. No one else can know how it behaves or what happens *in* or *to* it, except – indirectly – through that person's behaviour, which is not always a reliable indicator. Sometimes, even the person whose *chai* behaves in certain ways may not be aware of what is going on. All of this is demonstrated in idiomatic expressions such as *ru na mai ru chai* รู้หน้าไม่รู้ใจ 'know the face, cannot tell the *chai*', and *mai ru chai tua-eng* ไม่รู้ใจตัวเอง 'not knowing one's own *chai*'.

The dynamics of *chai* lead us to the following new components:

it can be like this: DYNAMICS

    when someone feels something good, something good happens in this part

    when someone feels something bad, something bad happens in this part many things can happen in this part when someone feels something

at the same time, it can be like this:

when someone feels something good, something good happens to this part

when someone feels something bad, something bad happens to this part

many things can happen to this part when someone feels something

this part can move

the same things can happen when someone thinks about something

other people cannot know what happens in this part

other people cannot know what happens to this part

มันสามารถเป็นอย่างนี้:   DYNAMICS

เมื่อคนคนหนึ่งรู้สึกบางสิ่งที่ดี, บางสิ่งที่ดีเกิดขึ้นข้างในส่วนนี้

เมื่อคนคนหนึ่งรู้สึกบางสิ่งที่แย่, บางสิ่งที่แย่เกิดขึ้นข้างในส่วนนี้

หลายสิ่งสามารถเกิดขึ้นข้างในส่วนนี้ เมื่อคนคนหนึ่งรู้สึกบางสิ่ง

ในเวลาเดียวกัน, มันสามารถเป็นอย่างนี้:

เมื่อคนคนหนึ่งรู้สึกบางสิ่งที่ดี, บางสิ่งที่ดีเกิดขึ้นกับส่วนนี้

เมื่อคนคนหนึ่งรู้สึกบางสิ่งที่แย่, บางสิ่งที่แย่เกิดขึ้นกับส่วนนี้

หลายสิ่งสามารถเกิดขึ้นกับส่วนนี้ เมื่อคนคนหนึ่งรู้สึกบางสิ่ง

ส่วนนี้สามารถเคลื่อนไหว

สิ่งเดียวกันนี้สามารถเกิดขึ้นเมื่อคนคนหนึ่งคิดบางสิ่ง

คนอื่นไม่สามารถรู้ว่าอะไรเกิดขึ้นข้างในส่วนนี้

คนอื่นไม่สามารถรู้ว่าอะไรเกิดขึ้นกับส่วนนี้

4.4 Control

There are a handful of components in the explication proposed in my earlier study (Svetanant, 2013) that I have not been able to place in any of the previous blocks. All other components, often significantly reworked, have been taken care of. Those that remain account for the control exerted by *chai* over the person as a whole. *Chai* is in absolute control, even when one does something "with" *chai* (cf. the saying *chai is the master, body the servant, referred to earlier*). Doing something with *chai* reveals one's true feelings or real intentions. They may be good, they may be bad. If someone cannot stay "true" to others, the reason is that this person's *chai* has become crooked, has doubled, or even multiplied, as attested by phrases such as *chai khot* ใจคด 'be deceitful' (lit. crooked *chai*), *song chai* สองใจ 'be torn between two lovers' (lit. two *chai*), and *lai chai* หลายใจ 'be flirtatious' (lit. many *chai*).

To account for the powers of *chai*, I propose a fourth block called *Control*:

if this part of someone is good, it is like this: CONTROL

    this someone cannot not do good things

    this someone cannot not feel something good towards other people

if this part of someone is bad, it is like this:

    this someone cannot not do bad things

    this someone cannot not feel something bad towards other people

ถ้าส่วนนี้ของคนคนหนึ่งดี, มันจะเป็นอย่างนี้:   CONTROL

    คนคนนี้ไม่สามารถไม่ทำสิ่งที่ดี

    คนคนนี้ไม่สามารถไม่รู้สึกบางสิ่งที่ดีต่อคนอื่น

ถ้าส่วนนี้ของคนคนหนึ่งแย่, มันจะเป็นอย่างนี้:

    คนคนนี้ไม่สามารถไม่ทำสิ่งที่แย่

    คนคนนี้ไม่สามารถไม่รู้สึกบางสิ่งที่แย่ต่อคนอื่น

Whether this is a block that will come in handy for the explication of other EPCs, only time will tell. It is proposed here as a possible expansion of Levisen's (2017) template.

4.5 Wrap-Up

The entire semantic explication of *chai* ใจ, represented both in English and in Thai, runs as follows:

someone's *chai* ใจ

something inside this someone   GENERAL CONCEPTUAL STATUS

this something is one of two parts of this someone

the other part is this someone's body

this part is not a part of this someone's body

this part is somewhere inside the left of the upper part of this someone's body

people cannot see this part

all people have this part

at the same time, it is like this: all living things have this part

because someone has this part, it is like this: CHARACTERISTICS

    this someone can live

    this someone can know many things

    this someone can think many things

    this someone can feel many things

it can be like this: DYNAMICS

    when someone feels something good, something good happens in this part

    when someone feels something bad, something bad happens in this part

    many things can happen in this part when someone feels something

at the same time, it can be like this:

    when someone feels something good, something good happens to this part

    when someone feels something bad, something bad happens to this part

    many things can happen to this part when someone feels something

    this part can move

the same things can happen when someone thinks about something

other people cannot know what happens in this part

other people cannot know what happens to this part

if this part of someone is good, it is like this: CONTROL

    this someone cannot not do good things

    this someone cannot not feel something good towards other people

if this part of someone is bad, it is like this:

    this someone cannot not do bad things

    this someone cannot not feel something bad towards other people

ใจ ของคนคนหนึ่ง

บางสิ่งข้างในคนคนนี้   GENERAL CONCEPTUAL STATUS

บางสิ่งนี้เป็นหนึ่งในสองส่วนของคนคนนี้

ส่วนอื่นคือร่างกายของคนคนนี้

ส่วนนี้ไม่ใช่ส่วนของร่างกายคนคนนี้

ส่วนนี้อยู่ในที่แห่งหนึ่งข้างในส่วนบนซ้ายของร่างกายคนคนนี้

คนไม่สามารถเห็นส่วนนี้

คนทั้งหมดมีส่วนนี้

ในเวลาเดียวกัน, มันเป็นอย่างนี้: สิ่งมีชีวิตทั้งหมดมีส่วนนี้

เพราะคนคนหนึ่งมีส่วนนี้, มันเป็นอย่างนี้:   CHARACTERISTICS

 คนคนนี้สามารถมีชีวิตอยู่

 คนคนนี้สามารถรู้หลายสิ่ง

 คนคนนี้สามารถคิดหลายสิ่ง

 คนคนนี้สามารถรู้สึกหลายสิ่ง

มันสามารถเป็นอย่างนี้:   DYNAMICS

 เมื่อคนคนหนึ่งรู้สึกบางสิ่งที่ดี, บางสิ่งที่ดีเกิดขึ้นข้างในส่วนนี้

 เมื่อคนคนหนึ่งรู้สึกบางสิ่งที่แย่, บางสิ่งที่แย่เกิดขึ้นข้างในส่วนนี้

 หลายสิ่งสามารถเกิดขึ้นข้างในส่วนนี้ เมื่อคนคนหนึ่งรู้สึกบางสิ่ง

ในเวลาเดียวกัน, มันสามารถเป็นอย่างนี้:

 เมื่อคนคนหนึ่งรู้สึกบางสิ่งที่ดี, บางสิ่งที่ดีเกิดขึ้นกับส่วนนี้

 เมื่อคนคนหนึ่งรู้สึกบางสิ่งที่แย่, บางสิ่งที่แย่เกิดขึ้นกับส่วนนี้

 หลายสิ่งสามารถเกิดขึ้นกับส่วนนี้ เมื่อคนคนหนึ่งรู้สึกบางสิ่ง

 ส่วนนี้สามารถเคลื่อนไหว

สิ่งเดียวกันนี้สามารถเกิดขึ้นเมื่อคนคนหนึ่งคิดบางสิ่ง

คนอื่นไม่สามารถรู้ว่าอะไรเกิดขึ้นข้างในส่วนนี้

คนอื่นไม่สามารถรู้ว่าอะไรเกิดขึ้นกับส่วนนี้

ถ้าส่วนนี้ของคนคนหนึ่งดี, มันจะเป็นอย่างนี้: CONTROL

 คนคนนี้ไม่สามารถไม่ทำสิ่งที่ดี

คนคนนี้ไม่สามารถไม่รู้สึกบางสิ่งที่ดีต่อคนอื่น
ถ้าส่วนนี้ของคนคนหนึ่งแย่, มันจะเป็นอย่างนี้:
คนคนนี้ไม่สามารถไม่ทำสิ่งที่แย่
คนคนนี้ไม่สามารถไม่รู้สึกบางสิ่งที่แย่ต่อคนอื่น

The NSM explications provided here, both in English (the language of investigation) and Thai (the language being investigated), offer a detailed and intuitively intelligible account of the meaning of the word, not only for cultural insiders but for cultural outsiders as well. The translation into Thai does not add anything that is not already there in the English version, nor does it leave anything out. It could have been first phrased in Thai, and then translated into English, and, again, nothing would have been either added or left out. Nothing else in linguistic semantics comes close to achieving this. Because the metalanguage that is used is universal (or at least near-universal), both in its lexicon and in its grammar, the resulting formulation in simple, culturally neutral, and cross-translatable words also provides a starting point for cross-cultural comparative research into the EPCs present in other languages.

5 Conclusion

There are a large number of heart-related lexical items in Thai, but the key cultural concept is the one that has been investigated here. The historical analysis undertaken in this study reveals that the primary conceptuality of the Thai EPC embedded in and embodied by the word *chai* has remained relatively stable since its first appearance in the 13th century. What has changed is the word's range of use, which has dramatically expanded. Originating in a Proto-Thai word meaning 'breath', *chai* is first used (in the Sukhothai period) to refer to a person's disposition; it represents a 'locus' where psychological activity occurs. The word maintains its original meaning throughout the centuries, but its occurrence in a steadily increasing number of metaphorical expressions and idioms, initially in the Ayutthaya period, later on in the Rattanakosin period as well, provides evidence of massive growth in cognitive and cultural salience. Thai people are born with *chai*; die at the very moment when *chai* departs the body; and, more than ever before, experience things with *chai*. *Chai* is a person's innermost secret part, linked to the body, but nowhere to be seen. *Chai* has a dynamic capacity to move around and change its shape, size, colour, or even temperature, depending on the circumstances.[9] While the English *heart* and *mind* were reshaped by the British Enlightenment (Wierzbicka, 1992: Chapter 1), the Thai 'heart', for the want of a better term, shows the influence of Buddhist beliefs according to which there is a *chai* inside all living things that takes over all mental/psychological activities regardless of whether they are emotional or intellectual: ใจเป็นนาย กายเป็นบ่าว *chai pen nai, kai pen bao* '*chai* is the master, body the servant'.

Acknowledgements

I would like to thank Bert Peeters, the editor of this volume, for his helpful comments and suggestions, and acknowledge the TNC and the http://vajirayana.org/ website as the source for most of the Thai excerpts used in this chapter.

Appendix A

Conceptual Metaphorical Chai ใจ *in* Lilit Phra Lo

Thai script	RTGS (Royal Thai General System of Transcription)	Meaning: Morpheme	Meaning: Compound
ติดใจ	*tit chai*	attach	like
ไว้ใจ	*wai chai*	put, keep	trust
เดาใจ	*dao chai*	guess	guess what one's thinking or feeling
หัวใจ	*hua chai*	head	physical heart
เต็มใจ	*tem chai*	be full	be willing to
ทันใจ	*than chai*	catch up with	as quickly as required
ร้อน(รน)ใจ	*ron (ron) chai*	be hot, be impatient	anxious
(ชม)ชื่นใจ	*(chom) chuen chai*	admire, praise	be happy, be refreshing
ตกใจ	*tok chai*	drop	be frightened
เผื่อใจ	*phue chai*	reserve for	keep oneself in reserve
เอาใจ	*ao chai*	take	please
กินใจ	*kin chai*	eat	be impressive
หมองใจ	*mong chai*	be dull	be gloomy

(Continued)

Thai script	RTGS (Royal Thai General System of Transcription)	Meaning: Morpheme	Meaning: Compound
เกรง(กลัว)ใจ	kreng (klua) chai	be in awe, be afraid of	have deference
ร่วมใจ	ruam chai	join	be united in mind
อายใจ	ai chai	be shy, be embarrassed	be ashamed
คาใจ	kha chai	get stuck	remain in one's mind
ขัดใจ	khat chai	go against	be offended
สุดใจ	sut chai	tip, end	wholeheartedly
วางใจ	wang chai	lay down	trust
หนักใจ	nak chai	heavy	be heavy of heart
คลายใจ	khlai chai	loosen	be relieved
ส่องใจ	song chai	look through	investigate thoroughly
ปลุกใจ	pluk chai	awake	stir up one's spirit
เสียใจ	sia chai	lose	be sad
พึงใจ	phueng chai	should	be fascinate with
ฝืนใจ	fuen chai	resist	act against one's will
พอใจ	pho chai	be sufficient	be satisfied
ชั่งใจ	chang chai	weigh	consider
เจ็บใจ	chep chai	hurt, ache	be heart-sick
ผิดใจ	phit chai	wrong	be estranged
แรงใจ	raeng chai	strength	inner strength
(ขืน)ข่มใจ	(khuen) khom chai	disobey, suppress	act against one's will
จอมใจ	chom chai	top, chief	sweetheart

Appendix B

Examples of Chai ใจ *Compounds in the Rattanakosin Period*

Thai script	RTGS	Meaning: Morpheme	Meaning: Compound
ใจอาวรณ์	chai awon	cling	be so attached that one does not want to be apart
ใจฉกรรจ์	chai chakan	sturdy	boldhearted, daring heart
ใจจืด	chai chuet	tasteless	unkind heart
ใจเจ็บ	chai chep	hurt	mentally hurt
ใจฟุ้งซ่าน	chai fungsan	muddle	restless heart

(Continued)

Thai script	RTGS	Meaning: Morpheme	Meaning: Compound
ใจปราชญ์	*chai prat*	philosopher	brilliant heart
ใจหาย	*chai hai*	lose	be stunned with fear
ใจจะขาด	*chai cha khat*	be about to torn	be dying for something
ใจร้าย	*chai rai*	fierce, cruel	evil-hearted
ใจช้ำ	*chai cham*	bruised	be distressed
ใจซื่อ	*chai sue*	sincere, honest	faithful hearted
ใจหวาด	*chai wat*	be scared	scared heart, worry
ดังใจ	*dang chai*	as	as one expects
เขินขวยใจ	*khoen khuai chai*	be shy	be bashful
เข้าใจ	*khao chai*	enter	understand
สบายใจ	*sabai chai*	comfortable	be relaxed
จับใจ	*chap chai*	grasp	touching
พรั่นใจ	*phran chai*	be terrified	worry
ดลใจ	*don chai*	realise	inspiring
ระบมใจ	*rabom chai*	bruised	continue to be painful
น้อยใจ	*noi chai*	few	feel neglected
ประโลมใจ	*pralom chai*	console	soothing
นอนใจ	*non chai*	lie down	be unconcerned
จนใจ	*chon chai*	poor	be baffled
จำใจ	*cham chai*	remember	be unwilling
ผ่อนใจ	*phon chai*	slacken	be relaxed
สอนใจ	*son chai*	teach	be edifying
ป่วยใจ	*puai chai*	sick	heartsick
น้ำใจ	*nam chai*	water	kindness, thoughtfulness
ด้วยใจ	*duai chai*	with, by	with love
ยั่วใจ	*yua chai*	seduce	tempting
ติดอกใจ	*tid ok chai*	attach to chest	be attracted
ไม่มีใจ	*mai mi chai*	no	merciless, have no love for
สำรวมใจ	*samruam chai*	calm	concentrate
เศร้าใจ	*sao chai*	sad	be sad
อนาจใจ	*a nat chai*	be pitiful	be pitiful
ร่ำคาญใจ	*ramkhan chai*	be annoyed	be annoyed
บันเทิงใจ	*banthoeng chai*	be joyful	be joyful
ขาดใจ	*khat chai*	torn	die, stop breathing
สาแก่ใจ	*sa kae chai*	as to	be satisfied
คู่ใจ	*khu chai*	pair	partner
ปลงใจ	*plong chai*	lay down	make up one's mind

Editor's Postscript: Thai Exponents of NSM Primes

Unlike the other contributors, Chavalin Svetanant illustrates the cross-translatability of NSM explications by formulating hers in English *and* in Thai. Thai exponents of the primes can be found in the following table. They were established by Svetanant herself, with reference to previous research undertaken by Diller (1994) and Mekthawornwathana (2010), updated and amended as necessary. Each category of primes is further subdivided as follows: the Thai exponents are shown first using the language's own script, then a transliteration using RTGS (cf. Endnote 1); the English exponents are mentioned last.

Semantic primes (Thai and English exponents), grouped into related categories

ฉัน, คุณ, คนคนหนึ่ง, บางสิ่ง~สิ่ง, คน, (ร่าง) กาย CHAN, KHUN, KHON KHON NUENG, BANG SING~SING, KHON, (RANG) KAI I, YOU, SOMEONE, SOMETHING~THING, PEOPLE, BODY	substantives
ชนิด~อย่าง, ส่วน CHANIT~YANG, SUAN KIND, PART	relational substantives
นี้~อย่างนี้, เดียวกัน, อื่น NI~YANG NI, DIAOKAN, UEN THIS, THE SAME, OTHER~ELSE	determiners
หนึ่ง, สอง, บาง, ทั้งหมด, มาก~หลาย, น้อย NUENG, SONG, BANG, THANG MOT, MAK~LAI, NOI ONE, TWO, SOME, ALL, MUCH~MANY, LITTLE~FEW	quantifiers
ดี, เลว~แย่ DI, LEO~YAE GOOD, BAD	evaluators
ใหญ่, เล็ก YAI, LEK BIG, SMALL	descriptors
รู้, คิด, อยาก (ได้), ไม่อยาก (ได้), รู้สึก, เห็น, ได้ยิน RU, KHIT, YAK (DAI), MAI YAK (DAI), RUSUEK, HEN, DAIYIN KNOW, THINK, WANT, DON'T WANT, FEEL, SEE, HEAR	mental predicates
พูด, คำ, จริง~ถูก PHUT, KHAM, CHING~THUK SAY, WORDS, TRUE	speech

(*Continued*)

ทำ, เกิดขึ้น, เคลื่อน (ไหว) THAM, KOET KHUEN, KHLUEAN (WAI) DO, HAPPEN, MOVE	actions, events, movement
อยู่ (ใน) (ที่แห่งหนึ่ง), มี (อยู่), เป็น~คือ (คนคนหนึ่ง/ ของสิ่งหนึ่ง) YU (NAI) (THI HAENG NUENG), MI (YU), PEN~KHUE (KHON KHON NUENG/KHONG SING NUENG) BE (SOMEWHERE), THERE IS, BE (SOMEONE/SOMETHING)	location, existence, specification
(เป็น) ของฉัน (PEN) KHONG CHAN (IS) MINE	possession
มีชีวิตอยู่, ตาย MI CHIWIT YU, TAI LIVE, DIE	life and death
เมื่อ~เมื่อไหร่~เวลา, ตอนนี้, ก่อน, หลัง, เวลานาน, เวลาสั้น, สักพักหนึ่ง, ชั่วขณะหนึ่ง MUEA~MUEA RAI~WELA, TONNI, KON, LANG, WELA NAN, WELA SAN, SAK PHAK NUENG, CHUANG KHANA NUENG WHEN~TIME, NOW, BEFORE, AFTER, A LONG TIME, A SHORT TIME, FOR SOME TIME, MOMENT	time
ที่~ที่ไหน~สถานที่, ที่นี่, บน~เหนือ, ล่าง~ใต้, ไกล, ใกล้, ข้างๆ, ข้างใน, สัมผัส THI~THI NAI~SATHANTHI, THI NI, BON~NUEA, LANG~TAI, KLAI (MIDDLE TONE), KLAI (FALLING TONE), KHANG KHANG, KHANGNAI, SAMPHAT WHERE~PLACE, HERE, ABOVE, BELOW, FAR, NEAR, SIDE, INSIDE, TOUCH	place
ไม่~ไม่ใช่, อาจจะ, สามารถ, เพราะ, ถ้า MAI~MAI CHAI, ATCHA, SAMAT, PHRO, THA NOT, MAYBE, CAN, BECAUSE, IF	logical concepts
มาก, อีก MAK, IK VERY, MORE	intensifier, augmentor
คล้าย~เหมือน KHLAI~MUEAN LIKE~AS	similarity

Notes: Exponents of primes can be polysemous, i.e. they can have other, additional meanings. Exponents of primes may be words, bound morphemes, or phrasemes. They can be formally, i.e. morphologically, complex. They can have combinatorial variants or allolexes (indicated with ~). Each prime has well-specified syntactic (combinatorial) properties.

Notes

1 Monosyllabicity is one of three essential features of Thai, together with tones (each syllable has a tone that carries lexical or grammatical meaning) and the lack of inflectional morphology (Thai is an isolating language with a very low morpheme per word ratio; grammatical roles are determined by lexical meaning and word order). Thai words are transcribed by the Royal Thai General System of Transcription (RTGS). Some authors transliterate *chai* ใจ as *jai*.

2 Several other culturally unique Thai EPCs are lexicalized by means of mostly polysyllabic Pali and Sanskrit loanwords, such as *jit* จิต, *mano* มโน, *hathai* หทัย, and *winyan* วิญญาณ (Kotkaeo, 1984: 184–185), which cannot be investigated here; they were brought in after the adoption of Indian Buddhism and Brahmanism via Khmer, the old Cambodia, during the Sukhothai period (Bowring, 1857).

3 *Duang* ดวง is the noun classifier not only for hearts but also for planets, stars, postage stamps, and lights.

4 There is no evidence of written Thai before the Sukhothai period. The Ayutthaya period ended in 1767, with the fall of the eponymous kingdom in the second Burmese-Siamese War. Within a year, King Taksin, previously known as Phraya Tak (the governor of Tak), established the short-lived Thonburi Kingdom (1767–1782) and relocated the capital from Ayutthaya to Thonburi, across the Chao Phraya River from the present capital, Bangkok. The few literary works produced during this period are not included in the present study.

5 The stele's authenticity has been questioned and is still subject to ongoing academic debate. While the majority of Thai scholars believe in its authenticity, some have argued that it may have been fabricated during the reign of King Mongkut in the 19th century.

6 The English translations are based on Griswold and na Nagara (1971).

7 The English translations are based on Reynolds and Reynolds (1982).

8 Reynolds and Reynolds (1982: 62) employ the word *mind* in their translation. They justify their choice, which goes against the fact that *chai* ใจ is semantically closer to 'heart', on the basis that "it is considered to be the seat of thought as well as feeling".

9 In contemporary Thai, *chai* ใจ *can also refer, much like the English word heart*, to a focal point or a central location. This semantic extension is an aspect of the word's diachronic development that we have deliberately overlooked since the focus of the chapter was on the EPC embodied by it.

References

Bowring, John (1857). *The kingdom and people of Siam: With a narrative of the mission to that country in 1855*, Vol. 1. London: Savill & Edwards.

Diller, Anthony (1994). Thai. In Cliff Goddard & Anna Wierzbicka (Eds.), *Semantic and lexical universals: Theory and empirical findings* (pp. 149–170). Amsterdam: John Benjamins. doi:10.1075/slcs.25.10dil

Diller, Anthony V. N., & Juntanamalaga, Preecha (1990). 'Full hearts' and empty pronominals in Thai. *Australian Journal of Linguistics, 10*(2), 231–255. doi:10.1080/07268609008599443

Griswold, Alexander B., & na Nagara, Prasert (1971). Epigraphic and historical studies no. 9: The inscription of Ramkamhaeng of Sukhothai (1292 A.D.). *Journal of the Siam Society, 59*(2), 179–228.

กฎแก้ว, วิสันติ์ [Kotkaeo, Wisan] (1984). ที่มาของคำบาลีสันสกฤตในภาษาไทย และคำไวพจน์ในภาษาบาลีสันสฤต [*Thima khong kham Bali, Sansakrit nai phasa Thai lae kham waiphot nai phasa Bali, Sansakrit / Etymology of Indic loanwords in Thai; includes synonyms in Pali and Sanskrit*]. Bangkok: Phrae Phitthaya.

Levisen, Carsten (2017). Personhood constructs in language and thought: New evidence from Danish. In Zhengdao Ye (Ed.), *The semantics of nouns* (pp. 120–146). Oxford: Oxford University Press. doi:10.1093/oso/9780198736721.003.0005

เมฆถาวรวัฒนา, ทัศนีย์ [Mekthawornwathana, Thasanee] (2010). บทวัฒนธรรมของการขอโทษในภาษาไทย [The cultural script of apologizing in Thai]. มนุษยศาสตร์สังคมศาสตร์ (มหาวิทยาลัยขอนแก่น) *[Humanities and Social Sciences (Khon Kaen University)], 27*(2), 28–50.

Moore, Christopher (1992). *Heart talk: Say what you feel in Thai* (2nd ed.). Bangkok: Heaven Lake Press.

Reynolds, Frank E., & Reynolds, Mani B. (Trans.) (1982). *Three worlds according to King Ruang: A Thai Buddhist Cosmology*. Berkeley, CA: Asian Humanities Press.

Svetanant, Chavalin (2013). Exploring personhood constructs through language: Contrastive semantic of "heart" in Japanese and Thai. *International Journal of Interdisciplinary Studies in Communication, 7*(3), 23–32.

Wichiarajote, Weerayudh (1984). *Thai Language: Spiritual Language, and the Development of the Spiritual Culture*. Research material used in the International Seminar of Human Science Research held at Srinakarinwirote University, Thailand.

Wierzbicka, Anna (1992). *Semantics, culture, and cognition: Universal human concepts in culture-specific configurations*. Oxford: Oxford University Press.

5   Exploring Old Norse-Icelandic Personhood Constructs with the Natural Semantic Metalanguage

Colin Mackenzie

1 Introduction

This chapter examines some aspects of the Old Norse-Icelandic personhood construct *hugr* 'mind, heart, courage' and outlines ways in which the Natural Semantic Metalanguage (NSM) approach can be used to develop our understanding of it. Like ethnopsychological personhood constructs (EPCs) in other languages, *hugr* plays an important role as a cultural key word in Old Norse-Icelandic. While sharing similarities with its analogues in other medieval Germanic languages, *hugr* represents a particularly North Germanic way of thinking about the person. Because of this, it has received scholarly attention from within different disciplines, including comparative religion, archaeology, and anthropology. All of these are, of course, dependent on a solid semantic analysis of the concept. Using words like *mind*, *heart*, and *soul* to describe *hugr* gives us a rough approximation of the concept, but inevitably obscures some of its features and imposes others upon it. What I want to demonstrate here is that NSM can be a useful part of the linguistic toolkit for exploring historical EPCs by allowing us to see past culture-bound English concepts like *mind*, *heart*, *spirit*, and *soul*.

First, I illustrate how NSM explications can give us a detailed and clear understanding of *hugr* that shows how it relates to the English words typically used to translate it. The notion of "cultural script" is introduced as well (for more on cultural scripts, see the editor's postscript). Second, I suggest that NSM explications can be a valuable tool in comparing concepts in closely related languages by looking at the relationship between EPCs and the body in Old Norse-Icelandic and Old English. Finally, I consider how explications and cultural scripts can be used to differentiate a variety of Old Norse-Icelandic phenomena that are frequently grouped together as examples of the belief in a 'free soul' concept. A brief overview of Old Norse-Icelandic personhood constructs is needed, though, to set the scene.

2 Old Norse-Icelandic EPCs

Old Norse-Icelandic was the language of the Viking world and is the ancestor of the modern-day Scandinavian languages (for overviews, see, e.g. Clunies Ross, 2000; McTurk, 2005). It is primarily known to us through a large corpus of indiscriminately preserved texts across many genres produced in Iceland from the early 12th to the 15th centuries, but often of uncertain dating and chronology. Although recorded several centuries later than other medieval Germanic languages (Barnes, 2005: 173), the texts are unique in preserving accounts of pre-Christian religion and traditions, which are only obliquely alluded to elsewhere. As such, Old Norse-Icelandic appears to offer a glimpse into Germanic beliefs that have been obscured by layers of Christian influence elsewhere. In addition to comparative study from a Germanic and Indo-European perspective (e.g. Eggers, 1957; Flowers, 1983; North, 1991), Old Norse-Icelandic material has also been compared to the circumpolar, shamanistic traditions found in mainland Scandinavia (e.g. Price, 2002; Tolley, 2009). However, notwithstanding these pagan cultural traditions, Old Norse-Icelandic literary culture was itself influenced by Christianity, which brought widespread literacy to Scandinavia, and by later European traditions, particularly Anglo-Norman romance literature (Barnes, 2000; Kirby, 2000; Rikhardsdottir, 2012).

The same variety of influences and traditions is seen in Old Norse-Icelandic's EPCs, too. There are features that are familiar from other Germanic languages, others that are unique to Old Norse-Icelandic, and others still that appear to share similarities with shamanistic concepts of the person. Like Old English and other medieval Germanic languages, Old Norse-Icelandic conceived of a part of the person located in the chest cavity that was involved in thinking, knowing, feeling, and wanting, and that was responsible for a sort of war-like, heroic attitude. In Old Norse-Icelandic, this concept was known as *hugr*; in Old English, as *mōd*. Although learned, brain-based medical theories were known in both cultures, these did not dislodge the main personhood construct from the chest (Mackenzie, 2014: 137–144; Lockett, 2015). The heart was the vital, animating organ that played an important and overlapping role in the two languages. Lockett (2011: 43–50) has suggested that, in addition to the heart, there may have been a life force concept operating across Germanic; in Old English, this concept was called *feorh*; in Old Norse-Icelandic, *fjǫr*. These words are rare, though, and the concept is obscure in our sources. Furthermore, apart from these shared Germanic features, both languages had a form of the Christian concept of the soul, introduced after their conversion.

The most unusual concept from a Germanic perspective is the *fylgja*, which appears to be a type of familiar spirit that typically took the form of an invisible animal (Mundal, 1974, 1993; Simek, 1993: 96). There is the possibility that this concept was associated with that of *hamingja*, something like a person's luck (Simek, 1993: 129).[1]

The concept of *fylgja*, as well as being distinct from the cultural model of the person in other Germanic languages, has been seen to link Old Norse-Icelandic to shamanistic concepts. The concept of a 'free soul' is a feature of shamanistic practice (Tolley, 2009: 168–169), and it has been argued that *hugr* and some other concepts function in this respect. There are a range of interpretations related to this phenomenon, some of which I address in Section 5, but common ones are that the *hugr* could take on another skin or shape called *hamr* (Raudvere, 2008: 241) and that it could leave the body in the form of breath, spun out like a thread by those skilled in the Norse form of magic, *seiðr* (Heide, 2006a, 2006b, 2006c).

Apart from *hugr* and *mōd*, both Old Norse-Icelandic and Old English have large numbers of synonyms with cognates across the Germanic languages. One approach to these words has been to see them as indicators of a multiplicity of EPCs in the Germanic past, which may have continued into the time of our recorded sources (Flowers, 1983; Phillips, 1985; North, 1991). For example, North (1991: 39–62) argues that *hugr*'s synonym *geð* and its Old English cognate *giedd* represent a type of 'poetic soul' that has features distinct from other EPCs. However, in the texts that we have these words are used almost exclusively in poetry for alliterative purposes. I take the view that the structural parallels between the Germanic languages point to one main EPC located in the chest rather than a series of different parts of the person (for similar interpretations, see Godden, 1985; Low, 2001; Lockett, 2011). This is borne out by the numbers. *Hugr*, like *mōd*, is lexically highly productive. The University of Copenhagen's *Dictionary of Old Norse Prose* (DONP) lists 682 instances across more than 75 phraseological constructions, with dozens of compound and derived words. By comparison, *geð* 'mind, wits, sense; liking, disposition' is recorded 28 times in DONP and occurs three times in Eiríkur Rögnvaldsson and Bergljót Kristjánsdóttir's (1996) corpus of sagas and tales of Icelanders, compared to 361 occurrences of *hugr*.

The semantic explications of *hugr* in this chapter are based largely on the research I carried out for my thesis (Mackenzie, 2014), which was informed by examining more than 1,600 occurrences of *hugr* across most of the surviving corpus of Old Norse-Icelandic literature. In my thesis, I discuss the slightly different conceptions of the role of *hugr* and the heart in Christian and romance contexts. However, the explications provided in what follows are intended to be general enough to give an impression of how *hugr* operated across Old Norse-Icelandic literature as a whole and to demonstrate how it differs from other historical and modern EPCs.

3 *Hugr* as Mind, Heart, and Courage

DONP lists five senses for *hugr*: (1) "mind, thought, consciousness, emotion"; (2) "state of mind, mood/temper"; (3) "love, affection, sympathy"; (4) "courage, boldness, battle-spirit"; and (5) "spirits (of powerful men), ?fetch". There are only four recorded occurrences of the last sense of which I am aware (Mackenzie, 2014: 86), and the dictionary notes that "a clear distinction between def. 1 and def. 3 is not always possible" (DONP, s.v. *hugr*). Space precludes giving a full lexicographical portrait of *hugr* in all its phraseological constructions. Instead, what I want to show is how NSM explications can be used to carve out the meaning of an EPC like *hugr* independently of *mind, heart, courage*, etc., and how they can provide a means of comparison with these and other similar constructs.

The explication of *hugr* I propose in this section is considerably more elaborate than the one in my earlier work (Mackenzie, 2014: 125), where no semantic template is used. Neither of the templates that have since been devised (Wierzbicka, 2016; Levisen, 2017) were in existence, and at any rate the length of the explication did not interfere with either its readability or its comparability. However, as more components were added, it became necessary to "mould" the explication into an appropriate form. Two courses of action were open to me: I could adopt one of the templates that had in the meantime appeared, or I could devise my own. I decided to pursue the latter course of action, building on my readings of the available literature. They suggested to me that, although EPCs are invisible and therefore likely to vary more in their categorization than concrete concepts, what we find in the world's languages is anything but unregulated diversity. There appear to be three main parameters of variation. The first is how EPCs relate to the body: where they are located, and whether they are thought of as a body part or as an entity of a different kind. The second is which cognitive, emotional, volitional, and other attributes are assigned to or associated with individual EPCs. The third concerns general characteristics, such as whether EPCs are thought of as active or passive, what happens in or to them, whether they are involved in interpersonal relations, whether they are thought of as "having a mind of their own", and so on. Each of the parameters is addressed in a different part of my template, and the three parts – called *Status and location*, *Attributes*, and *Dynamics* (the latter after Levisen, 2017) – are arranged in the order indicated earlier.

3.1 Status and Location of Hugr

Returning now to *hugr*, we can first of all confirm that, in terms of location, this fundamental Old Norse-Icelandic EPC refers to something that is clearly and persistently located in the chest, as shown in Example 1, a verse from the Eddic poem *Þrymskqviða*:

1   *Hló Hlórriða hugr í bríósti,*

   er harðhugaðr hamar um þecþi. (Neckel, 1962: 115)

   'Thor's heart [*hugr*] laughed in his breast,

   when he, stern in courage, recognized the hammer' (Larrington, 1996: 101).

What is less clear is how *hugr* was conceived of in relation to the body and *hjarta* 'heart' in particular. I return to this in more detail in Section 4; however, I do not think there is sufficient evidence to propose that *hugr* was thought to be part of the body (Mackenzie, 2014: 91–105). Instead of making this explicit, I include the component 'people cannot touch this part'. I also include a component 'people cannot see this part' as there is no evidence of people being able to see someone's *hugr* outside of the occasions where *manna hugir* 'men's *hugr* (pl.)' appear in dreams. Depending on the significance one wishes to attach to such dreams, this component could be modified to say 'when it is in this place, people cannot see this part'.

Overall, the following set of components are proposed for the *Status and location* block of the explication (the typographical layout is the one that has become conventional in NSM semantics):

someone's *hugr*

something inside this someone   STATUS AND LOCATION

this something is part of this someone

this part is inside the upper [m] part of this someone's body

people cannot see this part

people cannot touch this part

3.2 *Attributes*

Phraseological evidence identifies thinking and feeling as the most common attributes assigned to *hugr*, with a more limited role set aside for knowing. The components proposed in this subsection are intended to give an impression of the schema or semantic model of *hugr* that underpins and reinforces the phraseological evidence, and to show how it differs from *mind* and *heart*.

In contexts of knowing, *hugr* tends to be used in relation to a person's interpretation of events, i.e. in terms of what that person knows *about* something that happened. It is in that context that it compounds with *vit*, which is cognate with English *wits* and derived from the verb *vita* 'to know', and with *fróðr* 'wise' and *speki* 'wisdom'. In terms of thinking, on the other hand, *hugr* is used in phrases such as *koma í hug* 'come to mind, occur to one', *vera í hug* 'be in one's mind', *ganga/líða/hverfa ór hug* 'leave one's mind, forget', *snúa hug sínum eptir/at/frá* 'turn one's mind after/to/from', and others. *Hugr*'s role in thinking is further evidenced by the derived verbs *hugsa* 'to think upon' and *hyggja* 'to think, believe, intend, etc.'

Importantly, although it shares thinking and knowing with *mind*, *hugr* is different from *mind* in a number of respects. It does not seem to share the intellectual properties of *mind* and is not responsible for someone's *ability* to think or to know things, as *mind* is. Rather, someone thinks about things *with* one's *hugr*. Nor is it presented as the organ responsible for consciousness. Consciousness, intelligence, and understanding are instead associated with the aforementioned concept of *vit*. Comparing the compound and derivational vocabulary of the two words, *vit* and *hugr*, is instructive in this regard. Someone who is *huglauss* or *huglítill* is cowardly, whereas someone who is *vitlauss* is unconscious, mad, or drunk, and a *vitlítill* person is stupid. Similarly, a *hugmaðr* (*maðr* = 'man') is brave whereas a *vitmaðr* is clever (see entries in Zoëga, 1910; Cleasby & Vigfusson, 1957).

Summarizing this, I propose the following components should be included in the *Attributes* block of the explication:

because someone has this part, it is like this: ATTRIBUTES

    this someone can think some things

    this someone can know something about some things

A frequent phraseologism involving *hugr* in contexts of thinking and knowing is *segir hugr mér*, a fixed expression that means '*hugr* says to me', as in Example (2) from *Egils saga*:

2   "*Þat verðr <þá> allmjǫk á annan veg,*" *sagði Þórólfr,* "*en mér segir hugr um, því at ek ætla mik skulu af honum hljóta inn mesta frama*" (Einarsson, 2003: 6).

'"That is quite different from what I foresee," said Thorolf, "because I feel [lit. *hugr* says to me] I will earn great honour from him"' (Scudder, 2002: 9).

The phrase *segir hugr mér* '*hugr* says to me' often carries a sense of premonition. The same meaning is also expressed in the noun *hugboð* 'foreboding'. Strömbäck (1975) and Heide (2006a, 2006c) have argued, on the basis of later Scandinavian folklore, that these premonitions are evidence of someone else's *hugr* interacting with the person who has a *hugboð*. Both point to an incident in *Orkneyinga saga* where Sveinn Ásleifarson scratches his nose when he has a premonition that Haraldr Maddaðarson is making his way across the North Sea. Heide (2006c: 352) has argued that this itching is indicative of someone's *hugr*, expelled as breath, entering Sveinn's nose. As I have argued elsewhere (Mackenzie, 2014: 68–69), this goes beyond the evidence in contemporary sources. In *Orkneyinga saga*, as in almost all other examples of *hugboð* in the sagas and tales of the Icelanders (Rögnvaldsson & Kristjánsdóttir, 1996), this premonition is referred to with a personal pronoun. It is presented as someone's own thought, not a message received from another source. However, because of the role *hugr* plays in forebodings, we may want to rephrase the beginning of the *Attributes* block as follows:

because someone has this part, this someone can think some things ATTRIBUTES
at the same time, because someone has this part, it is like this:
this someone can know something about some things
sometimes, this someone can know something about something before other people can know it

So far, we have focussed on the cognitive aspects (knowing and thinking) of *hugr*. Because English segregates cognitive and emotional roles in its EPCs, *hugr* is translated as *mind* in some contexts and *heart* in others. However, this dichotomy does not exist in Old Norse-Icelandic; as DONP (s.v. *hugr*) notes, the 'mind' and 'love, affection, sympathy' senses are hard to distinguish. *Leggja hug á* 'lay one's *hugr* on' means 'think about something' in most cases, but it means 'fall in love with' when referring to a woman. Like *heart*, *hugr* is involved in feeling something good towards someone, but it does not have a moral character. One's *hugr* does not make one a good or bad person, nor is it naturally well disposed towards people, as English *heart* is (Goddard, 2008: 86). Instead, it varies according to circumstance.

Hugr is often used in a way that parallels English *mood*. It collocates with *góðr* and *heill*, and with *illr* and *grimmr*, in phrases roughly meaning 'to be in good or bad spirits'. However, these expressions are more commonly used interactionally; people feel good and bad things towards each other, as in Example (3) from *Laxdæla saga*:

3 *vænti ek, at þat sé auðvelt, því at flestir menn leggja góðan **hug** til þín.* (ÍF V: 211)

'I expect this would be easy, for most people are well disposed towards you [lit. lay a good *hugr* towards you]' (Magnusson & Pálsson, 1969: 225).

As well as feeling something good or bad towards someone, it also appears to be the case that *hugr* is involved in someone wanting to do something good for or bad to someone. This is expressed in the skaldic poem *Hákonarmál*:

4   *illúðigr mjǫk | þykkir oss Óðinn vesa; | séumk vér hans of **hugi**.*

'Óðinn appears to us [me] to be very hostile; we [I] fear his intentions' (Fulk, 2012: 189).

On the basis of what has been said, I propose the following components be added to the *Attributes* block of the explication:

when someone thinks about some things, this someone can feel many things
some of these things are good, some are bad
this someone can feel something good towards someone else
this someone can feel something bad towards someone else
this someone can want to do good things for someone else
this someone can want to do bad things to someone else

One final aspect of *hugr* we need to consider here is its role in martial courage. This particular aspect has been described as both an attitude (Quinn, 2012: 212) and a virtue (Haimerl, 2013: 43). Both are appropriate descriptions that indicate that someone's *hugr* enables them to think and act in certain ways that were valued in Old Norse-Icelandic culture.

Questioning someone's *hugr* forms the basis of insults, as in Example (5) from *Kjalnesinga saga*:

5   *Kolfiðr kallar þá ok mælti: "Ef Búi má heyra mál mitt, þá gangi hann ór einstiginu, ef hann hefir heldr manns **hug** en berkykvendis"* (ÍF XIV: 24–25).

'Then Kolfinn called out and said: "If Bui can hear what I am saying, and if he has the courage of a man rather than a she-beast, then let him come down this narrow path"' (Cook & Porter, 1997: 316).

Someone with a timid or fearful *hugr* is unable to act heroically, as depicted in Example (6), a verse by the poet Hjǫrtr:

6   *Munat í vári vestr langskipum*
    ***hugragr** of haf Haraldr fara.*
    Því mun lengi lafhræddr konungr
    alls andvani Englands ok vegs.

'Cowardly-minded Haraldr will not travel on long-ships west across the sea this spring. Therefore the terror-stricken king will long be bereft of all England and of honour' (Gade, 2009: 347).

Conversely, someone's *hugr* allows them to act bravely in battle, as Sigurðr the dragon-slayer says in the Eddic poem *Fáfnismál*:

7 **Hugr** *er betri, enn sé hiors megin,*

hvars vreiðir scolo vega (Neckel, 1962: 185)

'Courage is better than the power of a sword,

where angry men have to fight' (Larrington, 1996: 162)

To represent this aspect of *hugr* I propose to add the following to the explication:

because someone has this part, this someone can think like this:

"I know something bad can happen to me if I do things of one kind

I cannot not do things of this kind, I want to do things of this kind"

Acting with *hugr* is a default expectation of the prototypical Old Norse-Icelandic hero, best expressed in a cultural script instead of a social valuation component:

An Old Norse-Icelandic cultural script for inciting courage and bravery

people think like this:

it is good if someone thinks like this:

"I know something bad can happen to me if I do things of one kind

I cannot not do things of this kind, I want to do things of this kind"

it is bad if someone cannot do things of this kind because this someone cannot think like this

The first part of the cultural script underscores the virtue of thinking about acting with courage (or *hugr*); the second part emphasizes that acting in a cowardly manner is considered reprehensible, without saying that acting with *hugr* always leads to good outcomes.

3.3 Dynamics

Hugr's alleged ability to act independently of the body, as a 'free soul', will not be addressed here but is the topic of Section 5. This subsection deals with a few other dynamic features of the Old Norse-Icelandic *hugr* construct.

First of all, whereas little appears to happen inside the *hugr* of someone immersed in thought, contrary to what is argued to be the case in NSM explications of *mind* (Wierzbicka, 2016: 458; Levisen, 2017: 123), there are infrequent occasions where *hugr* is described as having something happen to it, or things happening inside it, when someone experiences good or bad feelings. The expression of emotion in the sagas is minimal, and, when it is mentioned at all, it is usually in reference to external bodily reactions, such as flushing, changing colour, shivering, sweating, or weeping (Miller, 1992; Wolf, 2014). There are infrequent references to *hugr* and *hjarta* burning with passion in Christian and romance texts, but in cases where we have the exemplars for translated texts, we can see that these have been minimized in Old Norse-Icelandic (Rikhardsdottir, 2012: 64; Mackenzie, 2014: 179;). Far more commonly, we have examples of *hugr* and the heart shivering in the chest. As an example, in Þórleifr jarlsskáld Rauðfeldarson's verse on the destruction of his ship, he states: *Hrollir hugr minn illa* 'my mind shivers badly' (Heslop, 2012). The contents of the chest moving and shivering is consistently associated with fear, and it is tempting to include this in the explication; however, because *hugr*, no matter how rarely, can be said to experience other sensations associated with other feelings, I think it is better to keep the explication general. I propose the following:

when someone feels something, something can happen to this part

because of this, this someone can feel that something is happening inside the upper [m] part of this someone's body

Second, although *hugr* speaks to people (see earlier), I do not think there is any evidence to suggest that it was thought of as being "like someone", i.e. an inner person with a "mind of its own", as Wierzbicka (2016: 463–469) has proposed for Augustine's *anima*, Hebrew *nepesh* and New Testament *psykhe*. There are occasions, particularly in Eddic poetry, as in the verse quoted in Example 1, where someone's *hugr* laughs. It could be argued that here *hugr* was thought to have more of a personality, as appears to be the case in Old English (Godden, 1985: 274). But unlike *mōd* in Old English, *hugr* is not presented as pleading with or petitioning the person, nor does it seem to want to do things independently of the person. Instead of saying that *hugr* was like someone, we could more neutrally phrase the meaning behind phrases such as *segir hugr mér* 'hugr says to me' as:

sometimes, when this someone thinks about something, this someone can think like this:

"this part says something to me about this something"

3.4 Summary

Bringing together the observations in Sections 3.1–3.3, we can now suggest the following explication for *hugr*, which can be used for comparative purposes:

someone's *hugr*

something inside this someone STATUS AND LOCATION

this something is part of this someone

this part is inside the upper [m] part of this someone's body

people cannot see this part

people cannot touch this part

because someone has this part, this someone can think some things ATTRIBUTES

at the same time, because someone has this part, it is like this:

this someone can know something about some things

sometimes, this someone can know something about something before other people can know it

when someone thinks about some things, this someone can feel many things

some of these things are good, some are bad

this someone can feel something good towards someone else

this someone can feel something bad towards someone else

this someone can want to do good things for someone else

this someone can want to do bad things to someone else

because someone has this part, this someone can think like this:

"I know something bad can happen to me if I do things of one kind

I cannot not do things of this kind, I want to do things of this kind"

when someone feels something, something can happen to this part   DYNAMICS

because of this, this someone can feel that something is happening inside the upper [m] part of this someone's body

sometimes, when this someone thinks about something, this someone can think like this:

"this part says something to me about this something"

Although not comprehensive, this explication demonstrates how *hugr* differs from English *mind* and *heart*, and how NSM can be used to explore historical EPCs without having to rely on target language concepts.

4 *Hugr*, the Heart, and the Hydraulic Model

The NSM methodology can also be used by historical linguists to present similarities and differences between concepts in closely related languages or cultures. To demonstrate the potential it has for contributing to this area of study I will compare the physiology of *hugr* to that of its Old English analogue *mōd*.

In Old Norse-Icelandic, interiority is rarely spoken about. This stands in stark contrast to Old English poetry, where there is a persistent focus on the inner life, to the extent that it effectively works as a structuring motif with a highly elaborated way of speaking about how thoughts and feelings interact with the body (Godden, 1985; Harbus, 2002; Lockett, 2011; Mize, 2013). Examples 8–10, taken from Lockett (2011: 60–61), give an indication of a prevalent motif which can be found throughout the corpus of Old English poetry:

8   *Ingelde / weallað wælniðas ond him wiflufan / æfter cearwælmum colran weorðað.*

'in Ingeld mortal hatred will boil up, and his love for his wife will become cooler in the wake of seething anxieties' (*Beowulf,* 2064b-6).

9 *breost innan weoll / þeostrum geþoncum, swa him geþywe ne wæs.*

'his breast seethed inside him with dark thoughts, as was not normal for him' (*Beowulf*, 2331b-2).

10 *Þær wæs wopes hring; / torne bitolden wæs seo treowlufu / hat æt heortan, hreðer innan weoll, / beorn breostsefa.*

'There was the sound of weeping; that faithful love, bitterly oppressed, was hot around the heart; the chest swelled inwardly; the mind-in-the-breast burned' (*Christ* B, 537b-40a).

This way of writing about *mōd*, its synonyms, and the emotions it conveys has frequently been interpreted from the perspective of conceptual metaphor theory, as it corresponds to the familiar metaphor emotion/mind is hot fluid in a sealed container (e.g. Low, 1998; Geeraerts & Gevaert, 2008). Lockett (2011), however, proposes instead to construe these examples as representative of an embodied physiological system that she refers to as the "hydraulic model". Lockett (2011: 62–63) argues that in Old English, the *mōd* was part of the body, understood to be the fleshy parts inside the chest cavity with the heart (Old English *heorte*) as its most central part. It would grow hot, boil, and swell in response to strong feelings. To release this pressure, the body reacted by expelling hot tears, words, and other things thought to be the contents of the chest. After this, with pressure reduced, the *mōd* would cool down and deflate. Lockett (2011: Chapter 3) draws on evidence from various cultures and languages to show that a version of this embodied, hydraulic system is common across the world. Whether this model was conceived of in metaphorical or physical terms in Old English is to some degree an intractable problem. Nonetheless, the representations of *mōd*'s relationship with cognitive and emotional processes in Old English can be presented in the following, partial explication that focusses on the dynamics of this EPC:

someone's *mōd*

something inside this someone   STATUS AND LOCATION

this something is part of this someone

this something is inside the upper [m] part of this someone's body

this someone's *heorte* [m] is part of this something

people cannot see this part

because someone has this part, this someone can think about   ATTRIBUTES
some things

when someone thinks about some things, this someone can feel many things

some of these things are good, some are bad

when someone feels something because this someone thinks   DYNAMICS
about something,

> many things can happen to this part because of this

it can be like this:

> this part is hot [m] for some time
>
> because of this, something happens to this part,
>
> like happens to water [m] when it is very hot [m]
>
> because of this, after this, this part is big for some time

because of this, this someone feels that something is happening inside the upper [m] part of this someone's body

at the same time, because of this, many things can happen to this someone's body

people can see some of these things, they cannot see all of these things

after this, because of this, it is like this:

> this something is not big anymore
>
> this something is not hot [m] anymore

This explication could be expanded and refined but, even in its present shape, it can serve to show how different *mōd* was to *hugr* in terms of its dynamics. It is easier to make the case that the *mōd* was thought to be part of the body because there is such a highly elaborated way of speaking about its role in somatic processes, which is absent in Old Norse-Icelandic.

Lockett (2011: 147) suggests that the hydraulic model seen in Old English exists in some form in Old Norse-Icelandic culture. However, when looked at as a whole, Old Norse-Icelandic in fact has very little in common with the Old English system (see Mackenzie, 2014: 107–123). Ironically, given the frozen volcanic landscape of

Iceland, which is effectively a geological version of Lockett's hydraulic model, heat is absent from the vernacular Old Norse-Icelandic psychological idiom (Mackenzie, 2014: 109). There are occasions of people's bodies swelling up in response to strong feelings, but these are rare (Mackenzie, 2014: 108). Instead, the main bodily expressions of emotion are blushing, tears, shivering, and changing colour. Even here there are notable difference. Tears are likened to hailstones, unlike the hot tears of Old English, and when people blush there is no reference to heat (Mackenzie, 2014: 112). There are infrequent cases of the language of heat being used in Christian and romance texts, as mentioned earlier, but there are no associated bodily reactions, and there is no causative interaction between the *hugr* and the body (Mackenzie, 2014: 109).

It may be that some form of hydraulic model operated in Old Norse-Icelandic ethnophysiology and ethnopsychology. However, unlike in Old English, it is not associated with the *hugr* or the *hjarta*. The hydraulic model and conceptual metaphor theory are useful ways of looking at the similarities between systems. However, they can hide a wide range of differences beneath these labels. Old Norse-Icelandic and Old English can both be considered as cardiocentric ethnopsychological systems in typological terms, but the relationship between the feelings inside the chest and how they interact with personhood constructs have been elaborated in very different ways. By presenting this physiology in terms of NSM explications, we are able to see just how different they are.

5 *Hugr* and 'Free Souls'

Hugr's apparent status as a 'free soul' is a topic of extensive discussion in the literature, presumably because, typologically, it is a relatively unusual feature of Western EPCs. What I want to argue in this final section of the chapter is that, while communicating something understandable, phrases like *free soul* can operate in the same way as words such as *mind, cardiocentric*, or *hydraulic model*; that is, they can obfuscate some conceptual features and facilitate others being read into the subject. I hope to demonstrate that NSM explications and cultural scripts can be used as tools to think about and present some phenomena that have been linked to the 'free soul' concept in a way that does not rely on concepts unattested in Old Norse-Icelandic literature.

Two phenomena in particular have been widely associated with
the concept of *hugr* as a 'free soul': shape-shifting and the atten-
dant animal spirits known as *fylgjur*. The relationship between
these and *hugr* has been used to inform interpretations of the Old
Norse-Icelandic form of magic *seiðr* and its apparent similarities
to circumpolar shamanistic traditions, where souls and spirits are
sent away from the body (e.g. Price, 2002; Heide, 2006a, 2006b,
2006c; Tolley, 2009). From the outset, it is worth noting that although *hugr* is associated with these in scholarly literature, the only
occasion where it appears as anything like a 'free soul' is in the
manna hugir episodes, where animals in dreams are referred to as
the *hugir* of men. There are no cases where *hugr* is mentioned in accounts of *seiðr* or shape-shifting (Tolley, 2009: 198). Instead, much
of *hugr*'s status as a 'free soul' is based on a puzzling kenning for
hugr referred to by the Icelander Snorri Sturluson in his guide to
skaldic poetry *Skáldskaparmál*, composed in the early 13th century
(Faulkes, 1998: xi). Part of his exposition of *hugr* is reproduced in
Example 11:

11 *Hugr heitir sefi ok sjafni, ást, elskugi, vili, munr. Huginn skal svá
kenna at kalla vind trǫllkvinna ok rétt at nefna til hverja er vill ok
svá at nefna jǫtnana eða kenna þá til konu eða móður eða dóttur
þess. Þessi nǫfn eru sér.* (Faulkes, 1998: 108)

'[Hugr] is called mind and tenderness, love, affection, desire,
pleasure. [Hugr] shall be referred to by calling it wind of troll-
wives and it is normal for this purpose to use the name of
whichever one you like, and also to use the names of giants, and
then refer to it in terms of wife or mother or daughter. These
names form a special group' (Faulkes, 1987: 154).

It has been taken from this that *hugr* was like someone's breath and
that it could leave the body (e.g. Weiser-Aall, 1936; Strömbäck, 1975;
Alver, 1989, inter alia). Something similar to this is seen in early
modern Scandinavian folklore, where witches are able to send out
their *hug* (descended from *hugr*) to harm and influence people and
things through illness and other means (Strömbäck, 1975; Heide
2006a, 2006b, 2006c). Quinn (2012) has argued that this kenning is
better explained as an expression for martial courage, rather than
a physiological description of *hugr*'s character. The arguments are
too involved to explore here, but it is worth noting that the kenning is not used in any way that parallels the *hug* of early modern

Scandinavian folklore (Motz, 1988; Frank, 1997). Even if one takes the 'wind of the troll women' kenning on face value, rather than as a reference to courage, it does not follow that *hugr* was conceived of as a 'free soul', able to leave the body.[2] Instead, this is inferred from a range of comparative evidence that deserves critical assessment.

5.1 Shape-Shifting

Raudvere (2008: 241) claims that *hugr* and *hamr* 'skin, form, shape' were Old Norse-Icelandic's "two fundamental terms for the human soul" and that shape-shifters were able to "propel their *hugr* into a temporary body or guise, *hamr*". While *hamr* is referred to frequently in these accounts, *hugr* is not.[3] There are two broad categories of shape-shifting in Old Norse-Icelandic literature (Ellis, 1943: 122–127; Grundy, 1998): one where someone changes their body into that of an animal, and another where someone either sleeps or enters a trance-likes state and operates elsewhere in animal form. The first category is rarer and is sometimes accomplished by putting on the skin (*hamr*) of an animal (Grundy, 1998: 104–106). This type of shape-shifting can be expressed in the following cultural script:

An Old Norse-Icelandic cultural script for shape-shifting (1)

people know it can be like this:

    sometimes, someone can do something

    when someone does it, something happens to this someone's body

    because of this, after this, it can be like this:

        this someone can be a creature [m] of another kind for some time

The second form of shape-shifting is more complex, as seen in the following passage from *Ynglinga saga*, which describes the god Óðinn's ability to change his shape:

12 *Óðinn skipti hǫmum. Lá þá búkrinn sem sofinn eða dauðr, en hann var þá fugl eða dýr, fiskr eða ormr ok fór á einni svipstund á fjarlæg lǫnd at sínum ørendum eða annarra manna.* (ÍF XXVI: 18)

'Óðinn changed shapes. Then his body lay as if it was asleep or dead, while he was a bird or an animal, a fish or a snake, and travelled in an instant to distant lands, on his or other people's business' (Finlay & Faulkes, 2011: 10).

A similar scene occurs in *Hrólfs saga kraka*, where a great bear is seen fighting for the Danish army. While this is happening, the hero Bǫðvarr bjarki is found motionless in the king's chamber away from the battle. He is roused by his companion Hjalti and agrees to join the battle saying:

13   *ek segi þér at sǫnnu, at nú má ek mǫrgum hlutum minna lið veita konunginum en áðr þú kallaðir mik upp heðan.*

'I tell you truly that I can give the king far less help now than before you called me away from here' (Tolley, 2007: 5).

Other examples of the same type are collected in Grundy (1998) and Ellis (1943). In some cases, the animals are invisible, and there are occasions where, when this other body is harmed, the person's human body suffers ill effects too. However, none give any indication of the mechanism whereby people accomplish these feats. All we are told is that the body is unconscious while the person acts in animal form elsewhere. I propose the following cultural script for this type of shape-shifting:

An Old Norse-Icelandic cultural script for shape-shifting (2)

people know it can be like this:

someone can do something

when this someone does it, something happens to this someone

because of this, after this, it can be like this:

this someone's body is like someone's body when this someone is sleeping [m]

at the same time, this someone can be somewhere else, not where their body is

this someone can be inside the body of another creature [m]

at this time, this someone can do many things with this other body as this someone wants

sometimes other people can see this body

sometimes other people cannot see this body

if something bad happens to this someone in this other place,

something bad can happen to this someone's body

Tolley (2007: 6) writes that, in the case of Bǫðvarr bjarki, we must take the apparition of the bear as an example of his 'free soul'.[4] However, 'free soul' is not a concept Old Norse-Icelandic has a word for. What I think is instructive in the previous script is that it can be composed without reference to 'part of this someone'. This accounts well for the description in *Ynglinga saga*, where Óðinn changes his *hamr* 'shape'. Of course, it may be the case that, during this form of shape-shifting, it was thought that 'part of someone' had or was inside another body but this is not expressed in the texts.

Ellis (1943: 123) writes that, in this form of shape-shifting, the body remains in one place while the 'conscious mind' is elsewhere. As we have seen, 'conscious mind' does not match the representation of *hugr* as an EPC. *Hugr* is not responsible for someone's thinking, but is the way a person thinks about things. This is a case where our assumption of how EPCs operate can lead us astray. Because English *mind* is responsible for consciousness, we might see these examples of someone's 'mind' operating elsewhere; however, this need not have been the case in Old Norse-Icelandic. Framing these cases as cultural scripts allows us to present them without having to use concepts like *mind* or *soul* and show where features of these concepts might be "read into" such phenomena.

5.2 Fetches

The second area of evidence used to support *hugr* being some form of 'free soul' comes from the Old Norse-Icelandic concept of *fylgjur* 'fetches'.[5] These have variously been described as a type of soul (Simek, 1993: 96), guardian spirits or attendants (Turville-Petre, 1964: 227), a kind of 'mirror' of the person (Tolley, 2009: 242) and other variations on this theme. I agree with Jakobsson (2013) that many of the "paranormal" or "supernatural" aspects of Old Norse-Icelandic culture are resistant to taxonomy, and that trying to pin them down may result in misrepresentation. However, describing *fylgja* and *hugr* and shape-shifting in terms of *souls* and *spirits* can lead to greater misunderstanding by enabling their various distinct features to be conflated. In the following, I present a minimal explication for *fylgja* that can be used to compare it to *hugr* and allow us to see the differences hidden beneath words like *soul* and *spirit*.

Although *fylgjur* are presented in a wide range of contexts and roles, there are some general features that unite them. Grundy (1998: 112) describes them as "a universally present, semi-independent being in the shape of an animal". As Ellis (1943: 129) points out, unlike in shape-shifting, the *fylgjur* operate independently of people. They appear to follow a person closely and to go ahead of them when they travel. They are rarely seen, and when they are it is either in dreams, by those with second sight, or by people just before their death. When they are seen, they take the form of an animal, whose appearance seems to imply something about a person's character or status (Mundal, 1993). In some cases, they appear in the form of women, though how these occurrences relate to the animal *fylgjur* is contested (Tolley, 2009: 226–229; Stankovitsová, 2015: 23). *Fylgjur* can interact and fight with each other, but there is no indication that they are controlled by the person with whom they are associated. They seem to be involved somehow in a person's fate, but it is not clear what mechanism underlies this. In the following explication, I use the component 'a being of one kind', as *fylgjur* do not appear to be a part of someone, but rather independent beings with a life of their own that are closely associated with a person. One could replace this component with 'part of this someone' or say that this being was 'like part of this someone', depending on one's interpretation. As a means of comparison with *hugr* and the shape-shifting cultural scripts, I propose the following provisional explication[6]:

someone's *fylgja*

a being of one kind

this being is near this someone at many times

at many times, people cannot see this being

the body of some beings of this kind is like a creature's [m] body

the body of other beings of this kind is like a woman's [m] body

beings of this kind can do many things to other beings of this kind

people know it is like this:

> sometimes, people can see this being for a short time

> when this happens, people can think like this:

>> "this someone is someone of one kind

>> I now know something about this someone

>> I know something will happen to this someone"

Even if one were to begin the explication with 'part of someone', it is clear how different this 'part of someone' is from *hugr* and how it differs from the cultural scripts for shape-shifting. There is no association with the body, with thinking, knowing, feeling, or wanting. These differences can be obscured by referring to *hugr, fylgjur*, and shape-shifting in terms of *souls* or *spirits*. However, there is one area where *hugr* and *fylgja* do clearly overlap. This is in the *manna hugir* passages, where people see animals in their dreams that appear to signify someone's hostile intention, as in the following passage from *Hávarðar saga Ísfirðings*, Chapter 20. Here Atli has had a disturbed sleep; when asked whether he dreamt of anything unusual, he responds:

14 *Ek þóttumk ganga út ór búrinu, ok sá ek, at vargar runnu sunnan á vǫllinn átján saman, en fyrir vǫrgunum rann refkeila ein. [...] En er þau váru komin heim at bænum, þá vakði Torfi mik, ok veit ek víst, at þat er manna hugir; skulum vér þegar upp standa.* (ÍF VI: 349–350)

'I dreamt that I walked out of the storehouse and I saw eighteen wolves running together from the south into the field, and in front of the wolves ran a vixen. [...] And just as they reached the farm, Torfi waked me, and I know for certain that they were the [*hugir*] of men. Let us get up immediately.' (Heinemann, 1997: 343)

To help us consider how the *manna hugir* incidents fit into the discussion of *hugr* as a 'free soul', I propose the following cultural script:

A cultural script for *manna hugir*

people know it can be like this

    sometimes, when someone is sleeping [m], this someone can see many creatures [m]

    this someone can think about it like this:

        "these creatures [m] want to do bad things to me"

    after this, when this someone is not sleeping [m] anymore, this someone can think like this:

        "some people want to do bad things to me"

    people can say what these creatures [m] are with the words *manna hugir*

Interpretations of the *manna hugir* episodes differ. Some, e.g. Dillmann (2006: 243) and Heide (2006c: 352), see them as examples of psychic attacks, where someone's *hugr* is sent out by someone skilled in magic. Others, such as North (1991: 109–110), see them as metaphorical representations of someone's intentions. Tolley (2009: 191) takes a middle line, seeing the *manna hugir* as a concession to Christian sensibilities, which would have looked unfavourably upon the representation of a pagan practice such as sending forth a 'free soul'. NSM cannot solve problems of interpretation of this kind. However, I suggest explications and cultural scripts *can* offer a tool for thinking about and comparing phenomena like *manna hugir, fylgjur*, and shape-shifting by clearly presenting where the similarities and differences lie.

Instead of thinking of these phenomena in terms of 'free souls' or other target language categories, it can be instructive to look at their shared semantic components. All share the component 'creature [m]' or 'creature's [m] body' but there is a great deal that separates them. In the second type of shape-shifting episodes referred to above, people are unconscious when in another animal form, whereas the *fylgjur* operate in animal form independently of the person. In the *manna hugir* incidents, people can see animals while they are asleep, but these differ from the shape-shifting animals that operate in the material world, not in dreams.

There was clearly a belief in Old Norse-Icelandic culture that people could change shapes and that they could act independently of the body. What is not clear is that *hugr* was thought to be involved in these processes. Using words like *soul* and *mind* to describe these phenomena can act like a solvent that allows a whole range of EPCs to dissolve, merge, and be used interchangeably. I am not arguing that this is always the case; however, what I would like to suggest is that, by exploring EPCs through semantic explications and cultural scripts, we can bring into sharp relief features that can be obscured by describing phenomena using target language concepts.

6 Conclusion

The degree of specificity used in NSM explications has been objected to in the context of historical semantics. Biggam (2012: 98), for instance, considers the precision of NSM as misplaced in a historical context and asks whether it is "sensible to express an incomplete and untestable historical concept in NSM when the whole ethos of this system is to 'get inside the head' of the (non-existent) native speaker". In light of the fact that historical semanticists are faced with the problems of incomplete and randomly preserved data and a lack of native speaker informants, Biggam considers the risk of misunderstanding historical concepts is too great to warrant using NSM. However, I would argue that the benefit of NSM to the historical semanticist is not that it lets us "get inside the head" of long deceased native speakers, but that it provides a well-developed metalanguage for explicating and comparing concepts in a stable and maximally culture-neutral manner.

What I hope to have shown in this chapter is that, rather than being impractical and potentially misleading, as Biggam (2012: 98) has suggested, NSM can be used fruitfully in historical semantics. I have shown how we can explicate the meanings of the Old Norse-Icelandic concept *hugr* without recourse to English words like *mind*, *heart*, and *soul*, and in a way that shows where the similarities and differences between these concepts lie.

Framing definitions in full NSM explications or cultural scripts may not always be practical or desirable. However, the principles of analysis behind these can act as a useful corrective to avoid ethnocentrism creeping into our interpretations of concepts from the past. In terms of the study of historical EPCs, I would suggest that replacing misleading terms such as *soul* and *spirit* with *part of a person* (or *part of someone*) and *being of one kind* would be an immediate practical benefit. However, I think there is much to be gained from using full NSM explications to facilitate comparative studies of historical concepts.

Acknowledgements

Many of the ideas in this chapter were developed during my PhD research, which was funded by the UK Arts and Humanities Research Council. I should like to acknowledge my thanks to the Council and to my supervisors at the University of Glasgow, Kathryn Lowe and Jeremy Smith. I should also like to thank Daria Izdebska and Catherine Mackenzie, as well as the two anonymous reviewers of this chapter, for their comments on an earlier version, and Bert Peeters for helping to refine aspects of the explications and cultural scripts presented in it.

Editor's Postscript: Cultural Scripts

Colin Mackenzie is the only contributor to the volume to propose *cultural scripts* as well as explications. Both use NSM, and both are attempts to capture what is culture-specific in terms that are semantically simple and readily cross-translatable. Cultural scripts (Goddard, 2009; Wierzbicka, 2015) are comparable to explications, but *what* they explicate is different. They do not explicate words or phrases, or concepts (such as EPCs), but they focus on cultural norms, i.e. widely shared ways of thinking about what it is good or bad to do, say, think, want, etc., in any given situation. Scripts usually start off with a phrase such as 'people think like this' (and variations on the same theme), and typically contain one or more statements of the type 'it is good if' or 'it is bad if'. In addition, it could be argued that, in some cases, cultural scripts articulate common knowledge; in this case, the introductory phrase would be of the type 'people know that it is like this' or 'that it can be like this'. The matter deserves more research. At any rate, in Mackenzie's chapter, both kinds of scripts are used.

Cultural scripts have sometimes been embedded in explications. I don't think that this is good practice. Levisen's (2017) semantic template for EPCs allows for a so-called *Social valuation* block to be added to its default tripartite structure (cf. Peeters, this volume). However, *Social valuation* is about what people think is good or bad; in other words, the *Social valuation* block is in fact a cultural script that should be removed from the template and articulated separately; alternatively, if it is to be linked to the template, it should be set off from the remainder through typographical means that go beyond the mere use of a caption. In his discussion of *hugr* and bravery, Mackenzie illustrates the former procedure.

Notes

1 A handful of other less frequent concepts that I do not discuss here are surveyed as 'soul' and 'spirit' terms by Tolley (2009).
2 Two other episodes from Norse mythology are sometimes used as evidence of *hugr*'s ability to leave the body. In the Eddic poem *Grímnismál*, the god Óðinn's ravens, which he sends out across the world each day, are named Huginn and Muninn, derived from *hugr* and a word for memory. There is also an episode in the mythological text *Gylfaginning* where Þórr's servant Þjálfi is outrun in a race by Hugi, again derived from *hugr*. The significance of these is discussed in Quinn (2012: 254).
3 There is an apparent, though difficult to interpret, pairing of *hugr* and *hamr* in stanza 155 of *Hávamál* (Mackenzie, 2014: 78–79).
4 Tolley (2007: 6–7) considers this motif to be a relatively recent borrowing into Old Norse-Icelandic from a nearby shamanistic society.
5 The standard work on this topic is Mundal (1974). Turville-Petre (1972) discusses possible changes in meaning. A useful recent overview is Stankovitsová (2015).
6 Habib (2017) has developed a semantic template for non-human beings that could be used to develop a fuller explication of *fylgja* and aid comparability with similar concepts.

References

Alver, Bente G. (1989). Concepts of the soul in Norwegian tradition. In Reimund Kvideland & Henning K. Sehmsdorf (Eds.), *Nordic folklore: Recent studies* (pp. 110–127). Bloomington, IN: Indiana University Press.

Barnes, Geraldine (2000). Romance in Iceland. In Margaret Clunies Ross (Ed.), *Old Icelandic literature and society* (pp. 266–286). Cambridge: Cambridge University Press. doi:10.1017/CBO9780511552922.012

Barnes, Michael (2005). Language. In Rory McTurk (Ed.), *A companion to Old Norse-Icelandic literature and culture* (pp. 173–189). Oxford: Blackwell.

Biggam, Carole P. (2012). *The semantics of colour: A historical approach.* Cambridge: Cambridge University Press.

Cleasby, Richard, & Vigfusson, Gudbrand (1957). *An Icelandic-English dictionary* (2nd ed.) by William A. Craigie. Oxford: Oxford University Press.

Clunies Ross, Margaret (Ed.) (2000). *Old Icelandic literature and society.* Cambridge: Cambridge University Press. doi:10.1017/CBO9780511552922

Cook, Robert, & Porter, John (1997). The saga of the people of Kjalarnes. In Vidar Hreinsson (Ed.), *The complete sagas of the Icelanders: Vol. 3* (pp. 305–327). Reykjavík: Bókaútgáfan Leifur Eiríksson.

Dillmann, François-Xavier (2006). *Les magiciens dans l'Islande ancienne: études sur la représentation de la magie islandaise et de ses agents dans les sources littéraires norroises.* Uppsala: Gustav Adolfs Akademien för Svensk Folkkultur.

DONP = *A Dictionary of Old Norse Prose/Ordbog over det norrøne prosasprog* (1983–). Copenhagen: Arnamagnæan Commission/Arnamagnæanske commission. Retrieved from https://onp.ku.dk/

Eggers, Hans (1957). Altgermanische Seelenvorstellungen im Lichte des Heliand. *Jahrbuch des Vereins für niederdeutsche Sprachforschung, 80,* 1–24.

Einarsson, Bjarni (2003). *Egils saga.* London: Viking Society for Northern Research.

Ellis, Hilda R. (1943). *The road to Hel: A study of the conception of the dead in Old Norse literature.* New York: Greenwood.

Faulkes, Anthony (1987). *Snorri Sturluson: Edda.* London: Everyman.

Faulkes, Anthony (1998). *Snorri Sturluson: Edda. Skáldskaparmál: Vol. 1.* London: Viking Society for Northern Research.

Finlay, Alison, & Faulkes, Anthony (2011). *Snorri Sturluson: Heimskringla: Vol. I: The beginnings to Óláfr Tryggvason.* London: Viking Society for Northern Research.

Flowers, Stephen E. (1983). Toward an archaic Germanic psychology. *Journal of Indo-European Studies, 11*(1/2), 117–138.

Frank, Roberta (1997). The unbearable lightness of being a philologist. *Journal of English and Germanic Philology, 96*(4), 486–513.

Fulk, Robert D. (Ed.) (2012). Eyvindr skáldaspillir Finnsson, *Hákonarmál* 15. In Diana Whaley (Ed.), *Poetry from the Kings' Sagas: Vol. 1. From mythical times to c. 1035* (p. 189). Turnhout: Brepols.

142   *Colin Mackenzie*

Gade, Kari Ellen (Ed.) (2009). Hjǫrtr, *Lausavísur 3*. In Kari Ellen Gade (Ed.), *Poetry from the Kings' Sagas: Vol. 2. From c. 1035 to c. 1300* (p. 347). Turnhout: Brepols.

Geeraerts, Dirk, & Gevaert, Caroline (2008). Hearts and (angry) minds in Old English. In Farzad Sharifian, René Dirven, Ning Yu, & Susanne Niemeier (Eds.), *Culture, body, and language: Conceptualizations of internal body organs across cultures and languages* (pp. 319–347). Berlin: Mouton de Gruyter. doi:10.1515/9783110199109.4.319

Goddard, Cliff (2008). Contrastive semantics and cultural psychology: English *heart* vs. Malay *hati*. In Farzad Sharifian, René Dirven, Ning Yu, & Susanne Niemeier (Eds.), *Culture, body, and language: Conceptualizations of internal body organs across cultures and languages* (pp. 75–102). Berlin: Mouton de Gruyter. doi:10.1515/9783110199109.2.75

Goddard, Cliff (2009). Cultural scripts. In Gunter Senft, Jan-Ola Östman, & Jef Verschueren (Eds.), *Culture and language use* (pp. 68–80). Amsterdam: John Benjamins. doi:10.1075/hoph.2.07god

Godden, Malcolm R. (1985). Anglo-Saxons on the mind. In Michael Lapidge & Helmut Gneuss (Eds.), *Learning and literature in Anglo-Saxon England* (pp. 271–298). Cambridge: Cambridge University Press. Reprinted (2002) in R. M. Liuzza (Ed.), *Old English literature: Critical essays* (pp. 284–314). New Haven, CT: Yale University Press. doi:10.12987/yale/9780300091397.003.0013. Page references are to the reprint.

Grundy, Stephan (1998). Shapeshifting and berserkergang. *Disputatio, 3,* 103–122.

Habib, Sandy (2017). The meanings of 'angel' in English, Arabic, and Hebrew. In Zhengdao Ye (Ed.), *The semantics of nouns* (pp. 89–119). Oxford: Oxford University Press. doi:10.1093/oso/9780198736721.001.0001

Haimerl, Edgar (2013). Sigurðr, a medieval hero: A manuscript-based interpretation of the "Young Sigurðr Poems". In Paul Acker & Carolyne Larrington (Eds.), *Revisiting the Poetic Edda: Essays on Old Norse heroic legend* (pp. 32–52). New York: Routledge.

Harbus, Antonina (2002). *The life of the mind in Old English poetry.* Amsterdam: Rodopi.

Heide, Eldar (2006a). *Gand, seid og åndevind.* PhD thesis, Universitetet i Bergen (unpublished).

Heide, Eldar (2006b). Spinning *Seiðr*. In Anders Andrén, Kristina Jennbert, & Catharina Raudvere (Eds.), *Old Norse religion in long-term perspectives: Origins, changes, and interactions* (pp. 164–170). Lund: Nordic Academic Press.

Heide, Eldar (2006c). Spirits through respiratory passages. In John McKinnell, David Ashurst, & Donata Kick (Eds.), *The fantastic in Old Norse/Icelandic literature: Sagas and the British Isles* (pp. 350–358). Durham: Durham University, Centre for Medieval and Renaissance Studies.

Heinemann, Fredrik J (1997). The saga of Havard of Isafjord. In Vidar Hreinsson (Ed.), *The complete sagas of the Icelanders: Vol. 5* (pp. 313–347). Reykjavík: Bókaútgáfan Leifur Eiríksson.

Heslop, Kate (Ed.) (2012). 'Þórleifr jarlsskáld Rauðfeldarson, *Lausavísur* 5'. In Diana Whaley (Ed.), *Poetry from the Kings' Sagas: Vol. 1. From mythical times to c. 1035* (pp. 375). Turnhout: Brepols.

ÍF V = Sveinsson, Einar Ól. (1934). *Laxdæla saga*, Íslenzk fornrit V. Reykjavík: Hið íslenzka fornritafélag.

ÍF VI = Þórólfsson, Björn K., & Jónsson, Guðni (1943). *Vestfirðinga sǫgur*, Íslenzk fornrit VI. Reykjavík: Hið íslenzka fornritafélag.

ÍF XIV = Halldórsson, Jóhannes (1959). *Kjalnesinga saga*, Íslenzk fornrit XIV. Reykjavík: Hið íslenzka fornritafélag.

ÍF XXVI = Aðalbjarnarson, Bjarni (1941). *Heimskringla I*, Íslenzk fornrit XXVI. Reykjavík: Hið íslenzka fornritafélag.

Jakobsson, Ármann (2013). The taxonomy of the non-existent: Some medieval Icelandic concepts of the paranormal. *Fabula, 54*, 199–213. doi:10.1515/fabula-2013-0018

Kirby, Ian (2000). The Bible and biblical interpretation in medieval Iceland. In Margaret Clunies Ross (Ed.), *Old Icelandic literature and society* (pp. 287–301). Cambridge: Cambridge University Press. doi:10.1017/CBO9780511552922.013

Larrington, Carolyne (1996). *The Poetic Edda*. Oxford: Oxford University Press.

Levisen, Carsten (2017). Personhood constructs in language and thought: New evidence from Danish. In Zhengdao Ye (Ed.), *The semantics of nouns* (pp. 120–146). Oxford: Oxford University Press. doi:10.1093/oso/9780198736721.003.0005

Lockett, Leslie (2011). *Anglo-Saxon psychologies in the vernacular and Latin traditions*. Toronto: University of Toronto Press.

Lockett, Leslie (2015). The limited role of the brain in mental and emotional experience according to Anglo-Saxon medical learning. In Alice Jorgensen, Frances McCormack, & Jonathan Wilcox (Eds.), *Anglo-Saxon emotions: Reading the heart in Old English literature, language, and culture* (pp. 35–51). Aldershot: Ashgate.

Low, Soon-Ai (1998). *The Anglo-Saxon mind: Metaphor and common sense psychology*. PhD thesis, University of Toronto (unpublished).

Low, Soon-Ai (2001). Approaches to the Old English vocabulary for 'mind'. *Studia Neophilologica, 73*(1), 11–22. doi:10.1080/713789805

Mackenzie, Colin (2014). *Vernacular psychologies in Old Norse-Icelandic and Old English*. PhD thesis, University of Glasgow. Retrieved from http://theses.gla.ac.uk/5290/

Magnusson, Magnus, & Pálsson, Hermann (Trans.) (1969). *Laxdaela saga*. London: Penguin.

McTurk, Rory (Ed.) (2005). *A companion to Old Norse-Icelandic literature and culture*. London: Blackwell. doi:10.1111/b.9780631235026.2004.x

Miller, William I. (1992). Emotions and the sagas. In Gísli Pálsson (Ed.), *From sagas to society: Comparative approaches to early Iceland* (pp. 89–110). Middlesex: Hisarlik Press.

Mize, Britt (2013). *Traditional subjectivities: The Old English poetics of mentality*. Toronto: University of Toronto Press.

144   *Colin Mackenzie*

Motz, Lotte (1988). The storm of troll-women. *Maal og Minne*, 31–41.

Mundal, Else (1974). *Fylgjemotiva i norrøn litteratur*, Oslo: Universitetsforlaget.

Mundal, Else (1993). Supernatural beings: Fylgja. In Philip Pulsiano & Kirsten Wolf (Eds.), *Medieval Scandinavia: An encyclopedia* (pp. 624–625). New York: Garland.

Neckel, Gustav (Ed.) (1962). *Edda. Die Lieder des Codex Regius nebst verwandten Denkmälern, Vol. 1: Text*, Heidelberg: Carl Winter.

North, Richard (1991). *Pagan words and Christian meanings*. Amsterdam: Rodopi.

Phillips, Michael J. (1985). *Heart, mind, and soul in Old English: A semantic study*. PhD thesis, University of Illinois (unpublished).

Price, Neil S. (2002). *The Viking way: Religion and war in late Iron Age Scandinavia*. Uppsala: Uppsala University, Department of Archaeology and Ancient History.

Quinn, Judy (2012). The 'Wind of the Giantess': Snorri Sturluson, Rudolf Meissner, and the interpretation of mythological kennings along taxonomic lines. *Viking and Medieval Scandinavia, 8*, 207–259. doi:10.1484/J.VMS.1.103199

Raudvere, Catharina (2008). Popular religion in the Viking age. In Stefan Brink & Neil Price (Eds.), *The Viking world* (pp. 235–243). London: Routledge.

Rikhardsdottir, Sif (2012). *Medieval translations and cultural discourse: The movement of texts in England, France and Scandinavia*. Cambridge: D. S. Brewer.

Rögnvaldsson, Eiríkur, & Kristjánsdóttir, Bergljót S. (Eds.) (1996). *Orðstöðulykill Íslendinga Sögur: Orðstöðulykill og texti*, Reykjavík: Mál og Menning.

Scudder, Bernard (Trans.) (2002). *Egil's saga*. London: Penguin.

Simek, Rudolf (1993). *Dictionary of northern mythology* (Angela Hall, trans.). Cambridge: D.S. Brewer.

Stankovitsová, Zuzana (2015). *"Eru þetta mannafylgjur": A re-examination of fylgjur in Old Norse literature*. MA thesis, Háskóli Íslands. Retrieved from https://skemman.is/bitstream/1946/20343/1/ZS_fylgjur_MIS.pdf

Strömbäck, Dag (1975). The concept of the soul in Nordic tradition. *Arv: Tidskrift för Nordisk Folkminnesforskning, 31*, 5–22.

Tolley, Clive (2007). *Hrólfs saga kraka* and Sámi bear rites. In *Saga book, 31* (pp. 5–21). London: Viking Society for Northern Research.

Tolley, Clive (2009). *Shamanism in Norse myth and magic: Vol. 1*. Helsinki: Academia Scientiarum Fennica.

Turville-Petre, E. O. G. (1964) *Myth and religion of the North: The religion of ancient Scandinavia*. Westport, CT: Greenwood Press.

Turville-Petre, E. O. G. (1972). Liggja fylgjur þínar til Íslands. In Gabriel Turville-Petre (Ed.), *Nine Norse studies* (pp. 52–58). London: Viking Society for Northern Research.

Weiser-Aall, Lily (1936). Hugrinn – vindr trollkvenna. *Maal og Minne*, 76–78.

Wierzbicka, Anna (2015). Language and cultural scripts. In Farzad Sharifian (Ed.), *The Routledge handbook of language and culture* (pp. 339–356). New York: Routledge.

Wierzbicka, Anna (2016). Two levels of verbal communication, universal and culture-specific. In Andrea Rocci & Louis de Saussure (Eds.), *Verbal communication* (pp. 447–482). Berlin: De Gruyter Mouton. doi:10.1515/9783110255478-024

Wolf, Kirsten (2014). Somatic semiotics: Emotion and the human face in the sagas and þættir of Icelanders. *Traditio, 69,* 125–145. doi:10.1017/S0362152900001938

Zoëga, Geir T. (1910). *A concise dictionary of Old Icelandic.* Oxford: Clarendon.

Contributors

Yuko Asano-Cavanagh is a Senior Lecturer in the School of Education at Curtin University, Perth, where she teaches advanced Japanese and Japanese semantics. Her research focusses on the semantics and pragmatics of Japanese as well as on cross-cultural communication. She is the author of several semantic analyses of Japanese cultural keywords, using the Natural Semantic Metalanguage (NSM) approach. Her most recent publications include "*Kawaii* discourse: The semantics of a Japanese cultural keyword and its social elaboration" (2017) and "Japanese interpretations of 'pain' and the use of psychomimes" (2016).

Deborah Hill is an Assistant Professor at the University of Canberra. She has conducted extensive field work with the Longgu community of Guadalcanal, Solomon Islands. Her research interests include the interface between language and culture, descriptive grammar, and semantics. She also works in the area of language and development. Her articles in *Oceanic Linguistics*, titled "Bride-price, baskets, and the semantic domain of 'carrying'" (2016) and "Counting by tens: Specific counting in Southeast Solomonic languages" (2018; co-authored with Paul Unger), explore the relationship between language and culture.

Colin Mackenzie is a primary school teacher in Scotland. He completed his MA, MPhil(R), and PhD in the department of English Language at the University of Glasgow, where he taught Old Norse-Icelandic and Old English. His PhD thesis *Vernacular psychologies in Old Norse-Icelandic and Old English* (2014) examined the differences between the ethnopsychologies of medieval Iceland and Anglo-Saxon England.

Bert Peeters is an Honorary Associate Professor at the Australian National University, Canberra, and an Adjunct Associate Professor at Griffith University, Brisbane. His main research interests are French linguistics, NSM, and language and cultural values. Publications include *Les primitifs sémantiques* (ed., 1993), *The lexicon-encyclopedia interface* (ed., 2000), *Semantic primes and universal grammar* (ed., 2006), *Tu ou vous: l'embarras du choix* (ed. with N. Ramière, 2009), *Cross-culturally speaking, speaking cross-culturally* (ed. with K. Mullan and C. Béal, 2013), and *Language and cultural values: adventures in applied ethnolinguistics* (ed., 2015).

Chavalin Svetanant is a Lecturer in Japanese Studies at Macquarie University, Sydney. Influenced by her multilingual background, including Thai as a native tongue, her research interests lie primarily in the area of cross-cultural communication, investigating the relationship between language, thought, and culture in comparative cultural contexts. Her major publications include "Exploring personhood constructs through language: Contrastive semantic of 'heart' in Japanese and Thai" (2013) and "What lies underneath a political speech? Critical discourse analysis of Thai PM's political speeches aired on the TV programme *Returning Happiness to the People*" (2017).

For Product Safety Concerns and Information please contact our EU
representative GPSR@taylorandfrancis.com
Taylor & Francis Verlag GmbH, Kaufingerstraße 24, 80331 München, Germany

www.ingramcontent.com/pod-product-compliance
Ingram Content Group UK Ltd.
Pitfield, Milton Keynes, MK11 3LW, UK
UKHW021424080625
459435UK00011B/150